A Life of Promise

Poverty, Chastity, Obedience

Consecrated Life Studies. Volume 1.

A Life of Promise

Poverty, Chastity, Obedience

by

Francis J. Moloney, S.D.B.

Michael Glazier, Inc.
Wilmington, Delaware

ABOUT THE AUTHOR

Francis J. Moloney, S.D.B., is an internationally renowned Johannine scholar. He teaches at Salesian Theological College, Australia, and he has lectured extensively. His books include *The Johannine Son of Man*; *The Word Became Flesh* and *Disciples and Prophets.*

First published in 1984 by Michael Glazier, Inc., 1723 Delaware Avenue, Wilmington, Delaware 19806

Library of Congress Card Catalog Number: 83-82088
International Standard Book Numbers:
Consecrated Life Studies series: 0-89453-379-7
A LIFE OF PROMISE: 0-89453-370-3

Cover design by Robert McGovern
Typography by Richard Reinsmith
Printed in the United States of America

In Memory

of

Fr. Edward Power, SDB

(1910-1982)

CONTENTS

Who will deliver me from this body of death?
Thanks be to God through Jesus Christ our Lord!
There is therefore no condemnation for those who are in Christ Jesus. For the law of Christ Jesus has set me free from the law of sin and death (*Romans* 7,28; 8,1-2).
For freedom Christ has set us free; stand fast therefore, and do not submit again to a yoke of slavery (*Galatians* 5,1).
It is not only erroneous, but a heresy, to hold that life in the army, the workshop, the court or the home is incompatible with devotion. Purely contemplative, monastic or religious devotion cannnot be practised in these callings; yet these are not the only kinds of devotion; there are many others suitable for those who live in the world and capable of leading them to perfection. Wherever we find ourselves we not only may, but should, seek perfection.
(St. Francis de Sales, *Introduction to the Devout Life*, Part I, chapter 3 [1609]).

PREFACE

In a major statement on the Religious life, the Council Fathers at Vatican II insisted that one of the main criteria for the post-conciliar renewal of Religious was to be "the following of Christ as it is put before us in the Gospel" (*Perfectae Caritatis*, 2). However, they went further than a simple statement of fact; they insisted that this particular criterion "must be taken by all institutes as the supreme rule" (*idem*). A glance back over the past eighteen years since the closure of the Vatican Council would show that a great deal has been done to attend to the other criteria for renewal indicated by the Council Fathers: a genuine study, understanding and appreciation of the charism of each Religious family, and a healthily critical "understanding of men, of the conditions of the times and of the needs of the Church" (*idem*). While we have not always been successful in our efforts in these areas, serious and sustained attempts have been made. The changes in dress, forms of government, apostolic involvement and attitudes to the role of the Religious in the Church are obvious, visible, results of such efforts. But what of "the supreme rule": the following of Christ *as it is put before us in the Gospel*?

It appears to me that insufficient attention has been given to this central issue. While it would be arrogant — and much too early — to attempt a full explanation of why this has been the case, I would like to mention three factors which may have contributed to such a situation. First, the return to the charism of the founder led Religious into all sorts of fascinating historical and apostolic investigations. It was so very close to the ultimate answer to a question that many were posing: what is the specific identity of our Religious family in the Church? There was a serious look at what each family was *doing* in the Church and in the world, attempting to repeat, in our own time, the uniqueness of a particular apostolic thrust which had its origins in the charismatic vision of the various founders. The same could be said for the reading of the signs of the times. Our analysis of the hopes and needs of mankind today, our attempt to "answer the ever recurring questions which men ask about the meaning of this present life and of the one to come, and how one is related to the other " (*Gaudium et Spes*, 4), has again led us to a serious consideration of what we must *do* to play an actively effective and relevant role among men and women in the Church and the world of today. These considerations are important, and must never be lost from sight. Nevertheless, our fascination with them could run the risk of leading us away from the real issue, "the supreme rule": the rediscovery of the person of Jesus of Nazareth, and the setting out on a journey along his way. A second difficulty which we must face is the contemporary reluctance to read the Gospels critically. Unfortunately, the critical reading of the Gospels seems to belong to either the specialist, with all the trappings of Greek, Hebrew and German scholarship, or the fanatical "drop the Gospel open and see what God is saying to you today" attitude which is unfortunately so common among certain enthusiastic groups. A third factor emerges from the reluctance to read the Scriptures critically. The Council has rightly made the following of Christ "the supreme rule", but when it is all said and done, there are as many impessions of just who Jesus was and is as there are believing Christians. Many are happy with a Johannine — Zeffirelli demi-God who moves gently through the Holy Land, surrounded by a group of adoring disciples as he gazes through them with penetrating blue eyes. Others identify him as the prototype of the South American freedom fighter, and they often make a selective reading of the Gospel of Mark the basis of such a model. Between these two models there is a third very popular image: Jesus as the founder of an infallible and "rock-like" Church. A selection is made from Matthew's famous "Peter-texts" (especially Matt. 16,16-18; 18,18 and 28,16-18) and the Lucan material on the twelve apostles (see, among many passages, the programmatic Lk. 6,13 and Acts 1,12-26). However popular and helpful such models might be, they are all unilateral, and blind to the much more disturbing reality of Jesus of Nazareth which stands behind them.

It would be unfair to claim that all the fault lay on the side of the Religious themselves. Far too often the people who have been given the opportunity to equip themselves for a genuine and serious understanding of the Gospels avoid the real issue. They manage to sidestep the urgent nature of such questions by losing themselves in word-games and literary techniques to such an extent that they become irrelevant. None of this is good enough. It appears to me that the renewal of the Religious life must be dominated by a more serious and sustained consciously programmed attempt to rediscover the Jesus of the Gospels, and to walk behind him, cost what it may. Some years ago I published a book, *Disciples and Prophets. A Biblical Model for the Religious Life* (New York, Crossroad, 1981). That work was an attempt to contribute to a rediscovery of some sort of authentically biblical model for the renewal of the Religious life. As such, it was more than an academic exercise. It was my attempt to show how a serious and critical approach to the Bible produces a challenge to the Religious life which must be faced. I made no claims to have provided all the answers, but closely following a line already initiated by J. M. R. Tillard, OP and J. Murphy-O'Connor, OP, I wished to raise the questioning finger of the Gospels, reminding myself and my readers of the age-old priority in an authentically Christian life: the supreme rule has always been and will always be "the following of Christ as it is put before us in the Gospel" (*Perfectae Caritatis*, 2).

It is now several years since I completed the manuscript of *Disciples and Prophets.* Since that time the story of those pages has been repeated time and again, but it never comes out exactly the same way. Each audience has its own sensitivity and the many searching questions aimed at me have repeatedly driven me back to the Gospels. Of course, the journey of my own life has also reached further into God's strange ways, and thus although what follows is in many ways the central section of my earlier study (pp. 85-129), it simply cannot be the same: "for the word of God is living and active, sharper than any two-edged sword, piercing to the division of soul, of joint and marrow, and discerning the thoughts and intentions of the heart" (Heb. 4,12). What follows is a biblical reflection upon the ideals of a life of poverty, chastity and obedience, about which so much has been written over the centuries. Why another book? My answer is simply that I am not happy with much of what has been said and written over the centuries. As a Religious I have always had an interest in the so-called "evangelical counsels" of poverty, chastity and obedience. I have also been trained to work as a professional biblical scholar. This created a situation where I found myself reading contemporary works on spirituality and the Religious life and listening to conferences or retreats where there was a continual misuse of certain biblical material. For example, I heard and read that Matthew's version of the story of the rich young man (Matt. 19,16-22) was a proof that there was a more perfect way of life (over and above the life of the *ordinary* baptised person) to be found in the observance of the counsels. Paul's suggestion in 1 Cor. 7,32-35 that the unmarried should remain so was similarly an indication that celibacy was a life-style which brought the celibate closer to God. I knew from my professional study of these texts within the wider context of the theology and structure of

Matthew or I Corinthians that such was not the case. Such an interpretation of the text has arisen, over the centuries, from a "piecemeal" interpretation of passages which have been quarried from the New Testament in such a way that it was soon forgotten that they originally had a place within the context of a wider argument.

Once this problem had been faced, others began to arise. There is certainly a different *form* of Christian life in the Church, founded by the fourth century monks and marked by a public living of poverty, chastity and obedience. But if these "vows" have their origins in the Religious life, then is it proper to speak of them as *evangelical*? In what way can we speak of the demands of the Gospel as *counsels*? Obviously, these are rhetorical questions. The call to poverty, chastity and obedience, although basic to the form of Christian life nowadays called Religious life, stands at the heart of *any* form of life which claims to be modelled upon the life-style of the poor, chaste and obedient Jesus of Nazareth. It is obvious that all Christians have been called to the perfection of love and that baptism has inserted us all into the mystery of a Church and a life of grace where this is made possible. The vocation to "walk behind", "to follow" (see Mk. 1,16-20) Jesus of Nazareth, poor, chaste and obedient, could not possibly be the special privilege of only *some* of the baptised. Again the Fathers of Vatican II have spoken boldly on the issue:

> The Lord Jesus the divine Teacher and Model of all perfection, preached holiness of life to each and every one of his disciples regardless of their situation... Thus it is evident to everyone that all the faithful of Christ *of whatever rank or status* are called to the *fullness* of the Christian life and to the *perfection* of charity (*Lumen Gentium*, 40. Stress mine).

The universal vocation to the fullness of the Christian life and to the perfection of love means that all — "of whatever rank or status" — are called to a radical commitment to the values of the Gospel, cost what it may. As this is the case, it is my opinion that we should not speak of evangelical *counsels*, as if they were something in the Gospels which may or may not be followed. Poverty, chastity and obedience — if they are Gospel values — are evangelic *imperatives* for all those who wish to follow Jesus of Nazareth, i.e. all the baptised. Naturally, there will be different *forms* of poverty, chastity and obedience, with the chastity of the celibate being the most public and striking of these different forms. Nevertheless, the biblical virtues of poverty, chastity and obedience are not the unique preserve of a small group of specialists in the Church; they are the touchstone of true Christianity, and thus of a true and authentic humanity: the poor, the chaste and the obedient are those called to the unique freedom which only the loss of self in love can hope to attain.

As a Religious, my little book will reflect my own experience, understanding and practice of poverty, chastity and obedience. However, it appears to me that it is vital for Religious to understand that their poverty, chastity and obedience *do not* place them in a class of their own, outside the Christian endeavour of the mainstream of the baptised in general. We have all been called to follow the poor, chaste and obedient Christ, be we Religious or not. Thus, even though many of my remarks and reflections in the pages which follow will be aimed, in the first instance, at my fellow-Religious, they are also written as a challenge to *all* the baptised, called to the uniquely poor, chaste and obedient way of Jesus of Nazareth. If poverty, chastity and obedience are Gospel values, then they must challenge all of us, as the Gospels were not written for Religious. They are a word of life and hope for all who claim to be followers of Jesus.

An earlier version of this book was published under the title *Free to Love: Poverty - Chastity - Obedience* (London, Darton, Longman and Todd, 1981). Michael Glazier's decision to republish it for an American public has given me the chance to rewrite the text completely, and rethinking the book has been a valuable experience. I am most grateful to Michael Glazier for offering me such an opportunity. The structure of each chapter is much the same. I attempt to raise the major problems which the virtues of poverty, chastity and obedience create in our contemporary world. Turning to the New Testament, I analyse our traditional texts critically, looking for the *original* message of the passage within its overall context, before applying it to our own situation. As a conclusion to each analysis of the biblical background for a life of poverty, chastity and obedience, I will attempt to make a few suggestions touching upon the manner in which the publicly professed "vows" of poverty, chastity and obedience in the Religious life can act as a prophetic challenge to all Christians, that all may realise their unique vocation to be followers of the poor, chaste and obedient Jesus of Nazareth.

This book is dedicated to one of the founding fathers of the Australian Salesian Province, my own Novice Master, a man whose recently concluded life-story has influenced the members of this Province more than any written word.

Francis J. Moloney, S.D.B.

Salesian Theological College
Oakleigh, Vic. 3166
Australia
31st January, 1983

POVERTY

There is a long-standing association between Christian virtue and "poverty". I have already suggested that biblical poverty should not be regarded as an evangelical counsel, something which may or may not be embraced by the Christian, but as an evangelical imperative. The indications are, therefore, that poverty is a good thing, but a reading of the Old Testament seems to tell another story. In the greater part of the literature of the Old Testament poverty is seen as a curse, and the blessings of Jahweh were always judged in terms of comfort, material success and wealth. This was part and parcel of the concrete approach to life which was typical of the Hebrew people. They seemed to care little for the philosophical; if Jahweh was pleased with them, then he blessed them with material wealth, victory in battle, and the many other benefits associated with a happy life here on earth. The contrary was the case when their infidelity and sinfulness aroused Jahweh's anger or jealousy. The book of Deuteronomy is dominated by this earthy approach (see, for example, Deut. 7,6-26). There were many reasons why such a belief was so central to the religious thought of the Hebrew people, but perhaps the most important was the lack of a theology of the after-life in earlier Hebrew thought.

One of the most striking examples of this principle is found in the experience of Job. At the beginning of the book of Job the hero is described as a man "who was blameless and upright, one who feared God, and turned away from evil" (Job 1,1). In this situation he is blessed with property, animals, household and a large family (see 1,3-5). However, all this is taken away from him, and Job continually sees such deprivation as clear evidence that God is displeased with him. So also do his various interlocutors who come to discuss his situation with him (see, for example, 6,8-13; 8,2-7; 19,2-22). A great part of Job's anguish arises from his inability to understand why Jahweh is so displeased. As is well known, he remains faithful and patient through it all, and thus, at the end of the story, Jahweh blesses him. It is interesting and important to notice that the blessings of Jahweh are again measured in terms of material abundance: "The Lord restored the fortunes of Job . . . and the Lord gave Job twice as much as he had before" (42,10. See also vv. 11-17).

Examples of this biblical attitude to wealth and possessions could be found throughout all the major books and traditions of the Old Testament. Particularly beautiful and impressive is the imagery of abundance, comfort and physical well-being which is used by the prophets to speak of the restoration of Israel after the humiliating experience of the Exile in Babylon (587-537 B.C.). This is especially true of the great prophets of that era: Ezekiel (see, for example, the famous visions of the dry bones in Ezek. 37 and the water flowing from the Temple in Ezek. 47) and Second Isaiah:

> Thus says the Lord:
> "In a time of favor I have answered you
> in a day of salvation I have helped you;
> I have kept you and given you as a covenant to the people
> to establish the land,
> to apportion the desolate heritages;
> saying to the prisoners, 'Come forth.'
> to those who are in darkness,
> 'Appear'.
> They shall feed along the ways,
> on all bare heights shall be their pasture;

they shall not hunger or thirst,
neither scorching wind nor sun shall smite them,
for he who has pity on them will lead them,
and by springs of water will guide them"
(Isaiah 48,8-10. See further chs. 54-55 and chs. 60-62).

The understanding of Jahweh as a God who saves and blesses *in fact* and not only *in words* is an important corrective to some of our current suggestions that the only authentic form of biblical poverty is to have nothing, to be reduced to a state of financial indigence. As I will have occasion to indicate, such an approach runs the risk of being too selective.

Nevertheless, as Israel came to a political and religious stage in her history when she was no longer master of her own property, wealth, possessions and political destiny, when all the material side of her existence seemed to be controlled by the foreign powers whose vassal she was, a spiritualisation of her thought naturally followed. It was no longer possible to see the saving hand of Jahweh in the fruits of the earth, the wine and food on the table, the children of a fruitful wife around the table, victory in battle and the beauty of Jerusalem. Where, then, could the saving presence of Jahweh be experienced? A most important feature of growth of Israel's religious thought happened at this stage of her political history (after the return from the Exile in 537): gradually there was the development of a belief in the after-life. The inevitable question arose: why do the wicked prosper and the virtuous starve? The answer had to be that Jahweh's blessings and punishments could not be measured by success or failure on this side of death. There must be some sort of further reward or punishment in the after-life. A most famous explicit confession of such a belief can be found in the well-known account of the slaying of the mother and her seven sons in II Maccabees 7, written, probably, in the last decade of the second century B.C. The second son defies his slayer with the words:

> You accursed wretch, you dismiss us from this present life, but the King of the universe will raise us up to an

> everlasting renewal of life, because we have died for his laws (II Macc. 7,9).

After seeing six of her sons slain, the mother continues to exhort the last and youngest of her children:

> Do not fear this butcher, but prove worthy of your brothers. Accept death, so that in God's mercy I may get you back again with your brothers (II Macc. 7,29).

A little before the writing of II Maccabees, in the midst of the persecution of Antiochus IV of Syria, the Book of Daniel appeared (about 165 B.C.). While the authors of the books of the Maccabees saw the solution to the sufferings of Israel in a military victory, Daniel went further, and saw that the only lasting solution was a religious one. Nevertheless, he also reflected the now-common idea of the after-life when he proclaimed:

> Many of those who sleep in the dust of the earth shall awake, some to everlasting life, and some to shame and everlasting contempt. And those who are wise shall shine like the brightness of the firmament; and those who turn many to righteousness, like the stars for ever and ever (Dan. 12,2-3).

This political and religious reaction to an experienced situation of poverty and oppression created a further development in the thought of Israel. It was no longer possible to claim that the rich and the powerful were blessed by God, for they were more often than not the violators of God's law. It was the humble, the suffering and the poor who were to be blessed. They came to be called "the poor of Jahweh", the *anawim*:

> I will remove from your midst
> your proudly exultant ones,
> and you shall no longer be haughty
> in my holy mountain.
> For I will leave in the midst of you
> a people humble and lowly.

They shall seek refuge in the name of the Lord,
those who are left in Israel;
they shall do no wrong
and utter no lies,
nor shall there be found in their mouth
a deceitful tongue.
For they shall pasture and lie down,
and none shall make them afraid (Zeph. 3,11-13).

It is very important, for our purposes, to notice that this widespread belief in the blessedness of the poor and the humble (see, for example, Pss. 22,24; 40,17; 69,33; 86,1-2; 109,22) did not lie in the mere fact of their being poor and oppressed. They were promised that they would be freed from such a situation. Their blessedness was to be found in their complete and profound openness to Jahweh. No longer did the faithful ones in Israel place their trust in the power of the sword and the shekel; they turned to Jahweh. In the light of their lack of political and economic strength, they were freed to love, and in that love they were promised a blessed future which only Jahweh could offer:

For they shall pasture and lie down,
and none shall make them afraid (Zeph. 3,13. See also Pss. 22,26; 40,17; 69,33; 86,12-13; 109,30-31).

This is the theme picked up by the New Testament, and especially by Luke, in its insistence that the Christian is called to poverty. Mary, the Mother of Jesus, is clearly presented as one of the *anawim*, as indeed are all the other major characters of the beautiful infancy stories of Luke 1-2: Zechariah, Elizabeth, Simeon, and Anna. Nowhere in the Bible is the attitude of the *anawim* so clearly stated than in Mary's response to God's demands:

I am the handmaid of the Lord,
let it be done to me according to your word (Luke 1,38),

and in her own explanation of why generations would call her blessed:

> He who is mighty has done great things for me,
> and holy is his name (Luke 1,49).

Luke then carries this theme further into his Gospel, through the preaching of Jesus, and even into the practice of the early Church, as we shall see. It is impossible for us to pause here to analyse why Luke made so much of this attitude, but a few indications of his use of the theme will show its importance. His version of the beatitudes states the theme clearly:

> Blessed are you poor, for yours is the kingdom of God.
> Blessed are you that hunger now, for you shall be satisfied.
> Blessed are you that weep now, for you shall laugh
> (Luke 6,20-21. Compare Matt. 5,3-6).

He insists that when the invited guests fail to appear, the poor from the highways and the byways must be invited to the banquet (14,15-21). Luke deliberately edits Mark's passage on the radical nature of discipleship in 14,25-33 (see Mark 8,36-9,1), adding an important further condition: "So in the same way, none of you can be my disciple unless he gives up his possessions" (v. 33. J.B.). Only Luke tells the story of the poor man Lazarus (16,19-31). However, it is not only Luke who has this idea. The importance of poverty did not begin with the third Gospel, as each one of the Gospels has it in its own way. The Marcan picture of Jesus is a powerful portrait of a man urgently pushing on to a God-determined destiny which leaves neither time nor opportunity for the gathering of possessions or the enjoyment of life's leisures. Even though Matthew has his own point of view, he follows Mark in this aspect of his Christology.

There can be little doubt that one of the major impressions left by the historical Jesus was that of a man completely overwhelmed by the "riches" of the Kingdom of God. Here it is that he placed his trust, and this is a key to a correct understanding of the Gospels' understanding of poverty. However, I must not rush ahead. Central to the traditional evaluation of evangelical poverty stands the story of the rich young man, a narrative which is found, with variations, in all three synoptic Gospels (Mark 10,17-22; Matt. 19,16-22; Luke 18,18-23). The tremendous ideal expressed in the words, "Go sell what you have and give to the poor, and you will have treasure in heaven; and come, follow me" (Mark 10,21; Matt. 19,21; Luke 18,22) stands at the heart of innumerable courageous attempts, down through the centuries of Christian history, to live a life of evangelical poverty. From St. Antony in the desert to Benedict in his monastery to Francis of Assisi on the road, and on into the founders and foundresses of our modern forms of the Religious life, this disturbing word of Jesus has provided the basis for what has come to be called "evangelical poverty". Despite the many practical difficulties which have always been involved in the literal observance of Mark 10,21, it could be shown that this expression alone has always provided a Gospel ideal for all forms of the Religious life.

From all that we have seen so far it could be said, therefore, that a life of poverty has ample support in the biblical tradition, in the lifestyle of Jesus of Nazareth, and in the history of Christian life. Our contemporary society, whose needs we must have continually in mind, also seems to be ready to listen to a valid message on the saving power of a life of poverty. Given the enervating affluence and the frantic search for the extra dollar that seems to mark our era, this could appear to be a strange affirmation. However, one does not have to look too deeply to notice that there is a deep dissatisfaction, both among the young and the not-so-young, with the slavery which our current search for material success is bringing about. This is becoming especially urgent in these days and months when the bubble is about to burst in our faces. Young people have been destroyed as they reached beyond themselves; families are broken apart, as the frantic search for that further advancement leaves love, hope and dreams out of the lives of people who were once full of love, hope and dreams. We live in a society which (to its detriment) often has little respect for the supposed "dehumanising" effects of chastity or for certain forms of obedience and authority, but many are opting out of a system which is run by the very small number of financiers who ultimately decide what happens in a capitalist society. There is a growing sensitivity to the fact that true freedom will *never* be found in the world's attractive offer of wealth, power and possessions. Whether we like it or not, we westerners of the eighties will have to face the reality of poverty and unemployment in a way that may even exceed the disastrous collapse of the great depression in the late thirties. Suddenly, poverty and how one copes with it have become urgent questions for our times.

Within this wider context we must try to understand the practice of a vowed life of poverty within the Religious life, and then see if such a practice has anything to say to Christians in general, as they attempt to live out their vocation to the evangelical imperative of Gospel poverty.

We have seen that poverty has a great deal of support from the Christian tradition: it is biblically based (although we must not forget the earlier Old Testament ideas), it appears to have been a part of the experience of Jesus, it has always been a part of the traditional structure of the Religious life in all its forms, and finally, it could well provide some sort of answer to the deepest and most urgent questions posed by contemporary men and women. Despite all of this, there can be little doubt that the practice of poverty in the Religious life today gives rise to a great amount of division and bickering, and is the source of many practical problems. This is already a serious matter in itself, as the witness value of any community which is torn apart by deep divisions over how poverty should be lived is greatly lessened. And not only does the community itself suffer, but also the local Christian community is greatly impoverished. However, even more serious than this is the anguish felt by a great number of sincere Religious who, struck by the suffering and pain of the impoverished millions of the world, and especially by the hopeless plight of those who are politically exploited, are often heard to say: "We are not really poor. We have plenty to eat, cars to move about in, a roof over our heads and a warm bed every night. More than this, we are not powerless. We have the means to fight our battles, and we are never exposed to the frightening insecurity about what 'tomorrow' might bring. All of these things are very much a part of what the world today calls 'poverty' — but they are not part of my experience". Although we have taken a vow called "poverty", it would appear that to insist upon this aspect of our lives is a dangerous double-talk. For the modern Religious to speak of being "poor" is nonsense. Having all the things we have and being basically secure about our 'tomorrows' within a world-wide context of more and more people who have little or nothing and live in the grip of a terrible uncertainty and insecurity, it would appear foolish to argue that we are poor. How deeply it can hurt when we hear the oft-repeated joke aimed at us by the non-Religious: "You take the vow of poverty . . . and we keep it!" It hurts because we all sense that there is a basis of truth in what is being said.

In the period of intense renewal which has gone on since Vatican II, coupled with the growing restlessness of the third world countries and a greater involvement and sensitivity among Christians to the injustice of such situations, this problem has become more and more urgent. It has also produced some wonderful initiatives among Religious. It is a stirring and prophetic reality that many Christians and many Religious are laying their very lives on the line — even to the point of death — to bring the person and message of Christ into these situations. Nevertheless, because of a lack of a serious consideration of what the Gospel has to say on the matter, I believe that a great deal of the anger, anxiety and confusion which we have all experienced has been unnecessary. There seems to have been two major attempts to solve this problem which, stated in their extremes, could be formulated as follows:

1. To speak of a vow of "poverty" today makes no sense. What is demanded of us, if we wish to remain faithful to this aspect of the tradition, is that we give ourselves wholly and generously to the task to be done in the Church and in the world. Given the political and emotional overtones that the

word "poverty" carries with it today, a different catchphrase is often used to sum up this aspect of our vowed life: poverty for the Religious means *availability*. This infers that while we make our contribution to the Church and to the world in our various apostolic and professional commitments, we are free to live, on the material level, like any non-Religious doing the same sort of work. What will be outstanding in the lifestyle of the Religious will be his or her availability. This point of view has become, in fact, the practice of many Religious — individuals and communities — in the more economically stable societies of the United States, Great Britain and Australia.

2. In complete contrast to the solution just outlined, there is a growing insistence that we return to a literal observance of the radical command of Jesus to the rich young man: "Go, sell what you have and give to the poor" (Mark 10,21). This means that the Religious in the Church must make a definitive option for the situation of the poor and the powerless, not just at the level of words and ideas, but at the level of practice. Large houses and the care and education of the wealthy must be abandoned; Religious communities must strip themselves of all worldly possessions and trappings so that they may really share the experience of those who are poor, powerless and exploited. It is especially important that the Religious share the experience of insecurity. Only in this way can they hope to play a significant role among the really poor. This attitude has been adopted in theory and in practice by many Religious — individuals and communities — in the extremely difficult situations of South America.

One must be careful not to scoff or rule out of court either of these attitudes (and the many variations and nuances of the same themes). There is much in them that can be of great value when it comes to the actual *practice* of poverty, i.e., the way in which some form of poverty has to be actually exercised. It may be true that we should be much more careful in our use of the word "poverty". This word has taken on considerable political, social and even emotional implications in our contemporary society which were never involved in the Latin *paupertas*, coined by the earliest reflections on the vowed life. It must also be said that availability has always been a most important aspect of the life of a committed Religious. It is one of the most outstanding signs of that radical openness to God's future which a Religious can show to the world. It is also certainly true that the urgent call to give power to the powerless and hope to the hopeless is a profoundly biblical call, and some of us may have to take the risk of sharing in the powerlessness and hopelessness on a material level in order to point to the Power and the Hope that can transform such situations. Nevertheless, in my opinion, both of these solutions fail as the ultimate answer to the problem of the sense and function of poverty within the context of the Christian and the Religious life. These suggestions are not wrong because they are radical. The Christian vocation is a call to a radical and energetic living of Gospel values, and it is here that I find the weaknesses of some of the new "absolutes" which are often bandied about. These suggestions have not gone back far enough into the true "roots" (the real meaning of the word *radical*) of the Christian life. They have become bogged down in an attempt to find an immediate and universal answer to something which is too mysterious for such definition. As such, they fall short of a whole answer by looking at the question of the "haves" and the "have nots". Ultimately, they are caught up in the causistry of *how* it is done.

One of the great problems with our reflections upon these mysteries is that we tend to theorise ourselves into irrelevancy. This little book is running precisely that danger. I would like the reader to bear with me — at this crucial stage of my analysis — and listen to the reflections of one of my own Australian Salesian confreres who is working in the hill-country of war-torn Latin America. Recently two of his catechists have been ruthlessly murdered. Grappling with the whole mystery of his presence as a consecrated Religious in such a situation, he wrote this own Province. I would like to share that with you.

"As I finally come round to writing once again, I find it

hard to know where to begin. So much has happened, so much has changed. We have gone from one crisis to another, with tragedy following tragedy — wholesale slaughter, senseless violence, indescribable torture: man's inhumanity to man. Utterly incredible is the extent of the depravity, the horrible cruelty at which we have arrived. Most of us will never know the depths of anguish and agony in the lives of thousands ...., the vast majority of whom are a gentle, peace-loving people, unwillingly drawn into this tragic situation — a people who ask no more than to be allowed to cultivate their crops and to live out their lives perhaps in frugality and material poverty, but in rich spiritual values and cultural heritage. Anything I could describe would fall far short of the reality, would be at best only a pale reflection of the lived experience. It seems that the devil himself is at large and that all the forces of evil have been let loose with a vengeance. How the words of the Psalmist and the Prophet Jeremiah come to life in a situation like this: they literally describe what we are living through —

> Lord, you sell your people for nothing, you make us like sheep for the slaughter.
> They have handed over the bodies of your servants as food to feed the birds of heaven.
> And the flesh of your faithful to the beasts of the earth; they have poured out blood like water ...
> No one is left to bury the dead; we are left in the depths of distress.
> Let my eyes run down with tears night and day, and let them not cease,
> For my people is smitten with a very grievous blow ...
> If I go out into the field: behold those slain by the sword ...
> Behold the disease of famine.
> Awake, Lord, for we are bowed to the dust, our bodies crushed to the ground.
> Rise, come to our help; redeem us for the sake of your love.

I have seen too much violence and terror, but nothing has affected me more closely and more deeply than the recent brutal killing of two exceptional catechists and helpers, both twenty-two years of age, married men with families, who were working with us full-time in the parish. While on their way to one of the parish centres, they were detained on the pretext of being guerrillas. We do not know all the details of their arrest and deaths, but know enough about what cruel and inhuman treatment suspected guerrillas receive to be able to imagine the terrible suffering they would have undergone. When we inquired through others what had happened, the answer was to this effect: 'Oh, those young fellows who work with the priests? We finished them off once and for all'".

After speaking at length about the lives of the two young men, he then turns to reflect upon the so-called "radical" solutions of some of the new "absolutes" in an almost angry, yet profoundly evangelical way:

"We can do much good, but also untold harm. Responsible leadership at all times, but especially in these explosive circumstances, requires us to consider the consequences of our ideas, to try to foresee where we are leading the people. There are those who have led the people on a course of action they themselves are unwilling to follow, whose consequences they do not understand, laying a burden on the people they themselves are unable to carry. Some have literally led the people to the slaughterhouse, themselves fleeing to safety. We should not ask more of the people than we ourselves are willing to give. There are those who have stirred up hatred and division amongst the people, who have promoted a class struggle, advocating violence as the only means of improving things, of righting the wrongs, the deep-seated injustices. To incite the people to violence is by far the easiest thing to do. Violence seems an effective and fast solution to a complicated situation, but how tragically wrong, resulting in the annihilation of the very people we are trying to save. There is so much killing going on in the name of God, in the name of justice, in the name of brotherly love. May God have mercy on us all. May he pardon our blindness, our impatience, our infidelity to the truth, our cowardliness. We have forgotten how to love. We have forgotten that we are all brothers."

In the light of his assessment of the situation, our anguished confrere turns to an evaluation of his own role, as a Christian, as a Religious:

"Struggling to understand, I came to see more clearly that Christ calls us to discipleship, to a radical giving of ourselves, of all that we are and have. He does not promise personal security. We can see quite clearly from the Gospels that Christ knew to what he was calling his disciples: he was well aware of the challenges they were to face. But call them he did, without excuses, without watering down the demands of discipleship. He taught them, encouraged them, sent them out, knowing full well what was in store for them. Moreover, he personally led the way. A Christian, following Christ's example, is not promised a sheltered life, a life free from problems. Nor does he seek suffering and danger for their own sakes. Rather, he lives his life in faithfulness to the demands of the gospel, aware of the consequences, and accepting these wholeheartedly, asking no more than that God's will be fulfilled in his regard . . .

"I now realise more fully that the length of our days is of little importance. It is the manner in which we pass our life that matters. God is good to us when he lets us live. He is also good to us when he calls us to die. He chooses us and blesses us in a special way when he calls us to die for his sake. This is an exceptional blessing, a closer sharing, a deeper identification with Christ.

"Although at times we may be tempted to think so, prosperity, success and freedom are no guarantee of God's blessing. Our faith enables us to see that at times God gives us a precious blessing in the form of a crushing cross. Bitter though it be, hurt though it may, it is nevertheless a real blessing. Our faith helps us to see deeper, to see further. Faith teaches us that for the most part we can only expect to see darkly, to understand partly, that we ought to walk with unlimited confidence in our Father who one day will reveal to us the reason why. Pray to God for us all. May he bring us peace soon."

This profound and moving reflection is neither the speculation of a desk-bound theologian, nor the raving of an apocalyptic visionary. It is the reasoned result of the experience of a sensitive, deeply involved and level-headed practitioner. Real-life experience has shown clearly that any solution which claims to have found an answer in the "haves" and the "have nots" is an illusion, and can lead to disaster. Many of the crises which we have experienced in our personal and community evaluations of our lives of poverty, and even the old joke about who really lives the vow of poverty, miss the whole point, as they arise from a vision of things which is too narrow. Once we are in touch with evangelical virtues, then we are moving in the area of faith. Such values can never be reduced to the measurable and the controllable, and here our letter-writer has touched the heart of the matter and the ultimate key to our problem: "Our faith helps us to see deeper, to see further. Faith teaches us that for the most part we can only expect to see darkly, to understand partly, that we ought to walk with unlimited confidence in our Father who one day will reveal to us the reason why." Now we are touching the heart of a genuinely *biblical* poverty: a modern-day experience of *anawim.*

To reduce evangelical poverty to availability must be a false step, as it loses touch with the radically evangelical call to evangelise through a public commitment to the biblical demands of poverty. Availability can be found among many good people and communities who lay no claim to be followers of Jesus. There must be something more to the biblical vocation to poverty, something profoundly and radically Christian which somehow cannot be exhausted by our availability.

The literal observance of Mark 10,21: "Go, sell what you have and give to the poor," also fails as the complete answer.

As I have already indicated, the radical nature of this challenge has fired the hearts of many outstanding men and women, both past and present. Nevertheless, it is my conviction that it falls short of being the complete description of evangelical poverty for two reasons. First, it is too selective. Mark 10,21 is not the only word of Jesus, or the only word in the Bible which addresses itself to the question of Christian poverty. This raises my second problem. Is it really about poverty at all, when this verse from a gospel story is analysed *within the context of the whole story*?

After this lengthy analysis of the situation, I must turn now to a more detailed analysis of the major biblical texts, those just mentioned and others which, in my opinion, produce for us a more comprehensive and satisfactory solution to the problem of the biblical roots of the evangelical imperative of poverty.

The Basic Premise: A Shared Life 'In Christ'

It is well known that Paul devotes very little time and space to reflections on the person, personality and experience of the historical man, Jesus of Nazareth. If we were to depend solely upon Paul for our information about the life of Jesus we would learn that:

a) he was "born of a woman", a Jew under the Law (Gal. 4,4)
b) he instituted some sort of ritual meal, within the context of his final meal with his disciples, which looked forward to the events of the days that were to follow for its sense (I Cor. 11,23-26)
c) he died, was buried, was raised, and was seen (I Cor. 15,3-5).

However, for Paul, that is enough. The social and economic situations of the Pauline communities are also very difficult to rediscover from a reading of his letters. We do know that the Jerusalem Church seemed to be struggling financially, as Paul turned to his communities to raise money to support the impoverished mother Church (see, for example, I Cor. 16,1-4). As we shall see, we have in this important Pauline initiative a practical example of the ideal of radical sharing of all that one has which seems to have been typical of the early Church's teaching. Beyond that, however, Paul has little to offer. It must be said that his letters provide little or no indication on the material side of life of Jesus of Nazareth or the early Church, except for that one instance: the collection for Jerusalem. This could lead one to conclude too rapidly that the Pauline literature has nothing to offer a biblical study of poverty. This would be a mistake.

At the centre of Paul's Gospel stands the story of a Jesus crucified but risen. To everyone who is prepared to lose himself in love and service unto death, this Jesus offers a newness of life which can be ours *now* (see, for example, Rom. 5,1-5; Gal. 4,4-7) as we participate — even on this side of death — in what Paul continually calls "life in Christ". The concept of the Christian life being a "life in Christ" is something which dominates Paul's thought. From a reading of Romans alone, one can find that almost every aspect of the Christian life is somewhere described as "in Christ". The Christian is baptised "in Christ" (Rom. 6,3), lives his every day life, greets people, has his glory and the life of the Spirit ... "in Christ" (see Rom. 6,11; 8,2; 9,1; 15,17; 16,3-10) forms "one body" with other Christians "in Christ" (Rom. 12,5) and has redemption and eternal life "in Christ" (Rom. 6,11). Although, at first sight, this may appear to be somewhat remote from any consideration of biblical poverty, I hope that you will eventually come to see that here we are touching the theological reality which stands behind any authentically biblical understanding of poverty.

There is a lot of scholarly discussion over the meaning of the Pauline expression "in Christ". This is understandable, as all scholars agree that it communicates, for Paul, what he understands to be the very heart of Christian life. For Paul, to exist as a Christian, to "be" a Christian in an active, committed way meant to live "in Christ". Sometimes scholars become too single-minded. Simply to study Paul's use of the expression "in Christ" is insufficient. It is sounder to range a little more widely, and look at some texts where he uses this central expression with some other famous images. Often Paul speaks of the Christian's "putting on Christ", and his "becoming a new man". Unfortunately, these expressions are taken as indicating some sort of mystical experience, or the moral improvement which must accompany baptism into Christianity. There is much more to it. There are two famous Pauline texts where the images of "in Christ", "putting on Christ" and "becoming a new man" are all used in close association with one another:

> As many of you as were baptised *into Christ* have *put on Christ.* There is neither Jew nor Greek, there is neither slave nor free, neither male nor female; for *you are all one in Christ Jesus* (Gal. 3,27-28).
> You have *put on the new man . . . where* there cannot be Greek and Jew, uncircumcised and circumcised, barbarian, Scythian, slave, freeman, *but Christ is all in all* (Col. 3,10. A.T.).

There are several important facts which must be seen and understood for a proper appreciation of these texts. First, they come from two quite different periods of Paul's life, and thus were written within the context of two quite different experiences. The Letter to the Galatians was probably written in 55 A.D., while Paul was in the full flood of his missionary activity. Colossians, commonly called a "prison letter", appears to have been written towards the end of his life, presumably some time in the early 60's. It is commonly recognised that between the younger and the later Paul there is a maturation and even an alteration in his thought. As we will see when we analyse I Cor. 7 in our following chapter, his thinking on the subject of the end time shifted quite seriously between the beginning and the end of his career. This, and similar developments, can be easily traced by a comparison of his earlier and later letters. As well as the difference in Paul's personal experience and situation, these two letters were written into two quite different communities, which had two very different problems. The Galatian community was running the serious risk of turning back to the protection of the Law and thus, according to Paul, losing the unique freedom which had been won for them through the death and resurrection of Jesus Christ (see Gal. 5,1). The Colossians seemed to be facing problems from a more speculative, libertine, syncretistic stream of Jewish thought (see, for example, Col. 2,8.16.18.21-23). Yet, despite these very important *differences* in place, time and argument, our two texts are clearly very *similar*. This is quite striking.

There can be no doubt, in the light of the above observations, that the argument treated in the two texts is absolutely central to Pauline thought, and will not allow any alteration or adaptation with the change of time and circumstances. Both texts share the lists of traditionally hostile groups: Greek and Jew, circumcised and uncircumcised, slave and freeman, male and female. It is important, in order fully to understand Paul's argument, to remember that in the first century these divisions were an accepted matter of fact. No one in his right mind would have suggested that people should not have been divided according to that list — but Paul did! Both of our passages, reflecting a central idea in Pauline thought (see also Rom. 10,12-13; I Cor. 12,12-13; Eph. 2,11-22), claim that these accepted divisions are finished in an entirely new situation into which the Christian has entered. Notice my reference to a "new situation". It appears that we have a reference to a new situation which is described as "in Christ", "in the new man", and both the Galatians and the Colossians are told that they have "put on Christ". Notice the spatial concept that seems to be involved. The "new situation" is not a new frame of mind or a change of attitude. Paul seems to claim that by becoming a Christian, the ex-Pagan or Jew has moved into a new "place". In the passage from Galatians Paul describes this new situation as a place where all constitute "one man", while in Colossians Paul goes further and explicitly says that "the new man" is a place *where* (Greek: *hopou*) there cannot be such divisions.

This may appear to be a difficult concept, but a little reflection on the situation of the earliest Christians should help to clarify things. It is not only Paul who has this idea. A sense of "motion" from one place to another is also found in a famous Johannine expression which almost defies translation. For John, true faith is "faith *into*" (Greek: *pisteuein eis*) Christ. It may be difficult in English, but it reflected the concrete experience of the earliest Christians. In fact, to become Christians they did, in practice, make a journey from one place to another, from one situation into another. They literally "crossed the road" from synagogue or temple into the Christian community. Once we see this, then the Pauline and the Johannine expressions which indicate that conversion into Christianity led the convert into a new sphere of existence can more easily be understood. The language used reflects a lived reality.

I hope that this fairly detailed analysis has made it clear that "life in Christ" is not a new set of moral habits or some sort of mystical experience. It is deeply rooted in the real life experience of the Pauline Christians. It referred to their new *sphere of existence*. To become a Christian, in the Pauline vision of things, meant to go away from one *place* into another *place*, where all the normally accepted barriers between men and women were brushed aside. What Judaism and Paganism saw as "normal" was regarded as impossible in the new situation of Christianity. Because of baptism the Christian found himself in an entirely new situation, where others formed an *integral* part. To spell this out more clearly: the Pauline notion of "life in Christ", Paul's central understanding of what it meant to be a Christian, is nothing less than an insistence that our very existence as Christians is not something which we personally possess; it is a radically new situation of life and love into which we enter through baptism into the Church. To be a Christian, therefore, means to participate in the lives of others, to share, to break down all the barriers which divide. It would have been impossible for Paul to imagine an *autonomous* Christian. For Paul, autonomy and Christianity would have been terms which contradicted one another. We exist and have our lives *as Christians* only in the profound openness to the sharing of life and love with other Christians. It is within this sphere of the sharing of life, where all divisions are eliminated, that we can justifiably claim to be living as Christians.

A little reflection upon our own situation will show that it must be this way. Not one of us became a Christian, entered into the wonderful mystery of Church and the life of Grace, under our own steam! This was given to us by people who, in their own turn, drawn by the gift of God's love, were prepared to share what they already enjoyed: our parents or the people who drew us by the quality of their own Christian lives into this shared life "in Christ". Once we are "in Christ", to use Pauline language, to abandon this sharing of life is to go "out" of the life which has the imitation of Christ's loving gift of self as its lifeblood. This means that one abandons Christianity, even if we happen to have our *private* Mass and Communion and live according to a literal observance of the commandments all our lives. I am not saying that such a person is not saved. That is another question. I am saying, however, that he or she is no longer a Christian, living in the heart of the love and freedom which is the result of a "life in Christ". "For freedom Christ has set us free; stand fast therefore, and do not submit again to the yoke of slavery" (Gal. 5,1).

This profound vision touches all aspects of the Christian life. No genuine Christian can live for himself because his very existence *as a Christian* would thus be lost to him. We have our Christian lives only in so far as we depend upon other Christians, only in so far as we continually give to other Christians and receive from other Christians. We are Christians, we exist as Christians in, through, for and because of other Christians. While the rest of the New Testament does not systematically work through a theology of "life in Christ" as Paul does, the various authors simply presuppose such a life as their first premise. We will see that it is fundamental to Luke's understanding of the Jerusalem community in the early chapters of the Acts of the Apostles, but there is an even more extraordinary agreement in all the New Testament literature that there is only one law in Christianity: the new law of love. It had to be so, as to love and to allow yourself to be loved is the only way in which human beings can hope to experience the reality which Paul calls "life in Christ": to be, to exist for the other. This is the only way to authentic Christian life: a mutual reciprocity and interdependence which knows no barriers.

Now that we have looked at the very roots of our Christian existence: matching perfectly the anguished call from Latin America for "a radical giving of ourselves, of all that we are and have", we can turn to examine some of the more classical passages in the New Testament which are commonly used as the basis for discussions of evangelical poverty.

The Poverty of the Jerusalem Church

We have already mentioned passingly that Luke's Gospel pays more attention to the question of poverty than the other Gospels. Writing into a situation of settled Churches in the Gentile mission, the evangelist devotes a lot of attention to the incompatibility between material ease, wealth, the unquestioning acceptance of human security and the following of Jesus (see, for example, Lk. 4,18-19; 6,20-26; 12,15-31; 16,9-15.19-31). However, the author of the Gospel of Luke wrote a two-volume work, of which the Gospel is only the first volume. The second volume in his single "story", which carries the reader from the birth of Jesus (Lk. 1-2) to Paul preaching fearlessly in Rome, the centre of the world (Acts 28,17-31), is the so-called Acts of the Apostles (see, especially the two prefaces: Lk. 1,1-4 and Acts 1,1-2). The first five chapters of the Acts of the Apostles are devoted to the experiences of the earliest Christian community in Jerusalem, in the immediate post-resurrection period. In ch. 6 the seven deacons are appointed to look to the needs of the Hellenists. The problems of a non-Aramaic speaking Church begin to emerge, and the gradual movement from Jerusalem to "Judea and Samaria and to the end of the earth" (Acts 1,8. See also Lk. 24,45-48) begins.

The portrait of the Jerusalem community has been traditionally used by writers and preachers as a model for the Christian ideals of unity, love and poverty. It has been particularly important in discussions of the poverty of the Religious because there is an insistence on the "handing in" of all goods. However, before we turn to an analysis of a few key passages from this section of Acts, a few introductory remarks must be made. First, and most important of all, we must recognise that Luke is presenting the Jerusalem Church of these chapters as a model for his own Church, as he writes to them in the early eighties of the first century. There can be little doubt that Luke was depending upon some good sources for the basic facts of his report, even though he was not personally present at that stage of the Church's story. Nevertheless, as he is using the unity of the Jersusalem Church as an *ideal* model for his own churches, it is clear that he has *idealised* the situation of those days considerably!

There is evidence that the situation was not quite so peaceful. Within the Acts of the Apostles itself there is the strangely violent story of Ananias and Sapphira (Acts 5,1-11). Paul tells of an occasion in Antioch where Peter seemed to be using double standards and drew forth the ire of Paul (Gal. 2,11-14). At a later stage Paul and Barnabas seem to have argued seriously over the suitability of John Mark as a companion on the second missionary journey (see the contrast between Acts 15,1-21 and 15,36-41). Barnabas, the senior man, Paul's guide and first companion, parts company from his former follower and is never heard of again. These are hints and slight indications that sin and division have *always* been present in *any* Christian community — even the first community in Jerusalem! As I have already indicated, Luke's idealisation of those earliest days is one of his main methods of both warning and exhorting his divided communities. Through the narrative of Acts 1-5 he tells them how things *should* be. Once this is clear, then we must cease reading those beautiful stories as the brute facts of history; they must be read for their theological and religious message. We will find that such a reading will bring the early chapters of the Acts of the Apostles much closer to us. It is one thing to marvel at the beautiful days of the early Church; it is another to see them as a perennial appeal to the Church to be one in faith, together in heart and soul (see Acts 2,44; 4,32).

This leads me to my second introductory remark. The portrait of the Jerusalem Church in the Acts of the Apostles was not written as a model for future Religious communities. Luke and the rest of the New Testament knew of no such phenomenon. Luke was using the Jerusalem Church as a model for his own local communities. The important theological message of peace, unity, love and a profound sharing at all levels which is at the heart of Luke's story-telling is a message for the whole Church. Nevertheless, Religious communities are, in their own turn, profoundly caught up in the mystery of the Church; they are "Church". They do not stand outside the universal Church. They belong to it, and Religious communities must reflect the quality of a life of love which is demanded of the whole Church (see the fine reflections of *Lumen Gentium*, 43-47 and the recent Roman document *Mutuae Relationes*, 1-4; 10-14). Thus, not only are we permitted to use the model of the Jerusalem Church in our reflections, which are aimed primarily at the Religious life, but we *must* use that model if we are to see clearly that *all* are called to the biblical imperative of the perfection of love, be they Religious or non-Religious, Priest, Brother, Sister or Nun, married or unmarried. Thus, even though these passages are often rightly used to appeal to Religious communities, they were not written for that purpose. They are directed to the Church. Thus, the message on "poverty", implicit within these narratives, is also directed to the whole Church.

We have just seen, from our study of the Pauline notion of life in Christ, that the Christian is never a Christian on his or her own. Our very lives as Christians depend upon our preparedness to share life. It is most important to notice, now that we are turning to the work of another author, in the Acts of the Apostles, that even though Luke never tries to work this out systematically, he makes it his basic point of departure. I would like to dwell briefly on the implications of two very important Lucan passages: Acts 2,44-45 and 4,32-35. Again a brief introductory note is necessary. As Luke tells his story, he repeatedly draws back from the events of the account itself to reflect upon the situation he is describing, to draw conclusions, or, as in the passages which we are about to analyse, to "summarise" what he has been attempting to communicate through his narrative. Scholars call these passages "redactional". They come entirely from the hand of the author, as he makes sure that the reader is led to the correct conclusions. This is very clear in the following passages. I will present them in parallels, as this will make it quite obvious that here we have Luke, the theologian and skilful writer, at work.

1) *And all who believed were together*	1) *Now the company of those who believed were of one heart and soul*
2) and had all things in common,	2) and no one said that any of the things which he possessed was his own, but they had everything in common . . .
3) --------	3) *There was not a needy person among them*
4) and they sold their possessions and goods	4) for as many as were possessors of lands or houses sold them, and brought the proceeds of what was sold and laid it at the apostles' feet;
5) and distributed them to all	5) and distribution was made to each

6) *as any had need* (Acts 2,44-45).	6) *as any had need* (Acts 4,32-35).

Luke makes his point with great clarity, and this carefully structured statement (2,44-45) and restatement (4,32-35) of the same themes must not be lost. As an all important Lucan "summary", they are vital for a correct understanding of the whole Lucan message in these early chapters of Acts. As far as our considerations are concerned, there are three central issues to be noticed:

a) Luke presupposes a unity of love which has been created by the new faith of the Jerusalem Church: "and all who *believed* were together (2,44); "now the company of those who *believed* were of one heart and soul" (4,32). Without this faith which produced a oneness among many, the rest of the passage would not make sense. Because the Christian faith of the community produces a situation parallel to that described by Paul as "life in Christ", the practical consequences follow logically. It is quite remarkable that Luke begins *both* his all-important "summaries" of the situation in the Jerusalem Church with two parallel statements on the unity of heart and soul which is the result of the community's commitment of faith.

b) Given the unity produced by such a faith, it must be seen that the first Christians are not portrayed as ridding themselves of all their wealth and possessions. On the contrary — they shared them! There is no hint of a suggestion in these texts that material things are intrinsically evil, and must be cast off if one wishes to become an authentic Christian. This is not even the point of the Ananias and Sapphira story, although that may appear to be the case, at first sight. A careful reading of these passages makes it clear that what happens is a sharing of the many goods and possessions which belong to the various individual members of the community — *to*

raise the standard of living of the needy members of the community (see 4,34: "There was not a needy person among them"). The goods are distributed to all those who were in need (see 2,45 and 4,35: "distribution was made ... as any had need"). The handing in to the apostles of all that one might possess has nothing to do with a disdain for the value of material things. On the contrary, it was done to ensure the comfort and material well-being of *all* the community. It must be stressed, at this stage, that the "handing in of goods" is not presented as an end in itself. It is not as if there is some special virtue involved in the actual handing in of the goods. If the *fact* of the handing in of goods is taken as the central message of the passage, we are led to believe that Luke's message is: if you want to be evangelically poor, in imitation of the Jerusalem community, you must hand in everything you possess to some local Christian leader. Such a solution would miss the point entirely, and absolutise the wrong issue. The handing in of the goods was only a means to an end, a method, and we must be careful not to absolutise a method and run the risk of losing touch with the reason why such a method was adopted. What is presented here has to be understood in the light of the faith which produced a unity of love: the earliest Christian community is presented as sharing all that it had as a sign of the love which each member had for the others, especially those most in need (see 2,45 and 4,35: "as any had need"). Because they loved with a new love, created by the new faith in Jesus as Saviour and Christ, they are presented as being committed to a very radical form of sharing. However, the handing over of the goods is only a visible, external, world-questioning consequence of a much deeper reality: the uniting and sustaining love which is the constitutive element in a Christian community — Paul's "life in Christ". Once this is clear, then the strange story of Ananias and Sapphira (Acts 5,1-11) is easier to understand. The couple is severely punished, not because they kept some of their goods. Peter makes it quite clear that they are perfectly free to do that in v.4: "While it remained unsold, did it not remain your own? And after it was sold, was it not at your disposal?" The sin of Ananias and Sapphira is that they *claim* that they have committed themselves to the radical unity of love through the total sharing of their goods, but *in fact* they are using this claim to hide their selfishness and avarice. This is serious, as the very essence of what it means to be a Christian is at stake; they are threatening the unity of mind and heart created by authentic faith. It is interesting to notice that we never hear reports from the early centuries of the Church's life that the non-Christians ever said: "See how these Christians hand in their goods". Apparently, the non-Christians were able to see through the external sign of the sharing of the goods, and to understand what was so startlingly new in a Christian community. They are reported as saying, with great wonder: "See how these Christians *love one another*" (Reported by Tertullian, *Apologeticum*, xxxix,7. Similar reactions are found in Minucius Felix and Lucian of Samosata. All reports come from the second century).

The sharing of goods must have made a serious impact upon those *outside* the Christian community. It would have been a gesture which forced the non-Christians to wonder what was the motivating force behind such human folly. In fact, Minucius Felix presents one Q. Caecilius Natalis exclaiming with ridicule: "They fall in love almost before they are acquainted" (*Octavius*, ix,2).

c) While the sharing of goods seems to have made an impact upon the world *outside* the community, leading it to read such a gesture as a sign of unqualified love, there must also be a further consequence to such action, profoundly affecting the people who are living their Christian lives *within* the community. Given the fact that the goods were shared by all, everyone, including the wealthy, now depended upon the community for their physical well-being. No longer do we have that situation of a subtle form of tyranny (so common along the many benefactors of our contemporary society) where some (the wealthy and the powerful) can dictate terms to the others (the poor and the powerless) by giving to them —and thus binding them even more tightly in the misery of their slavery. The subtle violence which has been perpetrated against the weaker nations of the Third World by the great powers is eloquent proof for the diabolic possibilities of such action. Obviously, this form of sharing has nothing to do with the freedom which Christ has come to bring. The message presented ideally by Luke, in his portrait of the original community in Jerusalem, is that *all* is *shared* by *everyone*. Such a situation *inside* a Christian community creates a life-style of mutual dependence and interdependence at a material level which reflects — at a much deeper level — the mutual sharing and reciprocity of "the life in Christ" which stands at the basis of all Christian existence and authentic freedom for humanity.

From our analysis of these important texts, we can see that the Lucan portrait of the Jerusalem community focuses its attention upon three fundamental questions:

1. Christian poverty springs from a genuinely Christian existence, a life in Christ, where faith has produced a deep desire to love and to break down the barriers of disunity. The Lucan passages pick up the earlier insistence of Paul, and translate it into narrative: "Now the company of those who believed were of one heart and soul" (Acts 4,32. See 2,44).

2. On a practical level, there is a placing at the disposal of the community of all that one has and all that one is. This becomes a world-questioning gesture, as those *outside* the community are led to conclude that such actions can only take place when they are motivated by love of an extraordinary quality.

3. Finally, there is a shared responsibility for the material life of the community. In this the community itself is forced to recognise that *no one* can call the tune within the Christian mystery of a unity created by faith and love. All of us are radically dependent upon others. This is the practical, lived experience of Paul's theological notion of a "life in Christ".

We have already examined the basic premise — life in Christ — in our study of the Pauline use of that term. We must turn now to give further consideration to the other essential elements of biblical poverty, as they have been presented in these texts from the Acts of the Apostles:

- The radical sharing with the community of all that one has and all that one is.
- The sharing within the community of the responsibility for the administration and care of all that is generated by its life together.

Giving the Community All That One Has

This aspect of Christian poverty is the one which causes most of us considerable difficulty. On the one hand, there is the tendency deep within each one of us to "possess". There are many areas of our lives which we want to guard, to make our own, and this easily spills over into the sphere of material things. The tendency to "possess" — at all levels — is perhaps one of the most disastrous effects of sin in contemporary society. On the other hand, many of us feel uncomfortable when we are faced with the proposal mentioned earlier: the *only* true way to Christian poverty is to follow to the letter the words of Mark 10,21: "Go, sell what you have and give to the poor". I have already indicated my own personal misgivings with this proposal, despite the support it has from the lives of some great men and women and the urgency of the demands of some contemporary movements within the Church and within Religious life.

From the very start one fact should be made clear. For the New Testament and, in fact, for the whole of the Bible, complete personal deprivation is *not* a good thing. We must never lose sight of the healthy attitude to God's blessings and subsequent material comfort as it is presented in the vast majority of the Old Testament traditions. This is also a *biblical* message, and stresses the very important fact that created things are good, created by a good and loving God and placed under man's care, for his use, development and mutual enrichment (see all of Gen. 1 for the *goodness* of creation and especially Gen. 1,26-31 for man's place within the goods of creation). Given that background, it should be obvious that the New Testament has no word of praise for personal deprivation, homelessness, hunger, nakedness, malnutrition, exploitation and powerlessness. All these things are the contradiction of the nature of the Kingdom of God, continually presented throughout both Old and New Testaments as the active reigning presence of a God who loves, as an experience of joy, peace, love, warmth, as a place where men and women are able to live with the dignity which is theirs because they are the creation of a loving, caring God. Indeed, we are the very image of that God (Gen. 1,26). The Bible speaks of freedom for the captives, health for the sick, food for the hungry, and the images of wedding feasts and an abundance of wine, food and all good things are constantly used (see, for example, Is. 58,6-9; 61,1-4; Amos 9,13; Hos. 14,7; Jer. 31,12; Mk. 2,22; Matt. 8,11; 22,1-14; Lk. 4,16-21; 22,16-18). How, then, have we come to the position, standing at the heart of that nagging feeling of guilt that disturbs so many sincere Religious (and also many successful lay people who have not faltered in any way in their faith), that we are not evangelically poor?

As I have already suggested, this difficulty flows from an uncritical and mistaken interpretation of the Gospels, especially the beatitudes and the story of the rich young man. A closer examination of these much used and abused texts should produce different results.

The Beatitudes

The beatitudes have come down to us in two quite different versions, in Luke 6,20b-26 and Matt. 5,3-12. As one or other of these versions can be taken up and absolutised as *the* beatitudes, I will give both the Matthean and Lucan versions in parallel:

Matt. 5,3-12	*Luke 6,20b-26*
3. Blessed are the poor in spirit, for theirs is the kingdom of heaven.	20b. Blessed are you poor, for yours is the kingdom of God
4. Blessed are those who mourn, for they shall be comforted.	
5. Blessed are the meek, for they shall inherit the earth	
6. Blessed are those who hunger and thirst for righteousness, for they shall be satisfied.	21. Blessed are you that hunger now, for you shall be satisfied. Blessed are you that weep now, for you shall laugh.
7. Blessed are the merciful, for they shall obtain mercy.	
8. Blessed are the pure in heart, for they shall see God.	
9. Blessed are the peacemakers, for they shall be called sons of God	

10. Blessed are those who are persecuted for righteousness' sake, for theirs is the kingdom of heaven	
11. Blessed are you when men revile you and persecute you and utter all kinds of evil against you falsely on my account.	22. Blessed are you when men hate you, and when they exclude you and revile you, and cast out your name, on account of the Son of man!
12. Rejoice and be glad, for your reward is great in heaven, for so men persecuted the prophets who were before you.	23. Rejoice on that day, and leap for joy, for behold your reward is great in heaven; for so their fathers did to the prophets.
	24. But woe to you that are rich, for you have received your consolation.
	25. Woe to you that are full now, for you shall hunger. Woe to you that laugh now, for you shall mourn and weep.
	26. Woe to you, when all men speak well of you, for so their fathers did to the false prophets.

This comparative reading of the two texts shows that each version reflects the interests and the literary skills of each evangelist. Matthew (5,1-2) situates his sermon on a mountain, where Jesus, as the new and perfect Law-*giver* takes over and perfects the role of Moses, who *received* the Law on a mountain, Sinai. Luke (6,12-20a) has Jesus, initially, on "the mountain" (v. 12) devoting the whole night to prayer. He then chooses and names his twelve apostles (vv. 13-16). He then comes down from the mountain, in the company of his apostles, and stops at a "level place" (v. 17), where he is totally available to all those who are afflicted. They come to him from all the regions to be cured, to touch him and to receive something from the power which comes forth from him (vv. 18-19). Matthew then arranges the beatitudes into two lists and a conclusion. There is first a series of four beatitudes which speak of passive attitudes (Matt. 5,3-6), followed by a second series of four beatitudes dealing with a more active thrust (5,7-10). He then concludes his list with the long beatitude (vv. 11-12) speaking very directly to the experience of his own community. It is also important to notice that, in a comparison with Luke, Matthew has spiritualised and generalised the demands of the beatitudes. Luke's beatitudes are more immediate and fiery, as is obvious from his use of the second person plural (you!). Most scholars would agree that the Lucan version is a closer reflection of Jesus' own preaching. However, Luke's skill as a writer is still in evidence through the careful balancing of four beatitudes (Lk. 6,20b-23) and four "woes" (6,24-26).

It is Luke's urgent linking of the underprivileged with the Kingdom (as against Matthew's "poor in spirit") that has led many contemporary movements and their writers to look exclusively to the Lucan beatitudes for biblical support. The arguments runs as follows. The Lucan beatitudes promise a fulfillment which the messianic era will bring for the underprivileged:

> Blessed are you poor, for yours is the Kingdom of God
> Blessed are you that hunger now, for you shall be satisfied
> Blessed are you that weep now, for you shall laugh (Lk. 6,20-21).

The passage can be read as a beatification of the state of being poor and oppressed; only to people who are actually caught up in the physical experience of poverty and suffering has the Kingdom of God been promised. Nothing is said of others, except to condemn the rich, the surfeited, those who can laugh and those of whom men speak well in the "woes" of vv. 24-26. The Kingdom, therefore, is the exclusive possession of the underprivileged.

This is a misreading of the text and a misplacing of the emphasis. Such an interpretation is only possible if the Lucan beatitudes are read as if they were the only things that Jesus said, or that Luke reported. Every text must be read within its overall context, both within the biblical literature as a whole, and especially, within the literary and theological structure of the document within which it is found. According to biblical thought, the Messiah was not coming to establish a situation of poverty, hunger and tears. The Messiah was expected to free men and women from such a situation, which is an offence against both God and humanity (see Qo. 4,5-6; Exod. 22,21-27; Deut. 15,11; Is. 58,6-7). This is a common theme in the Old Testament, and, as is his way, Luke continues this theme, and shows that all the hopes of Israel have been fulfilled in the person of Jesus of Nazareth. In Luke's Gospel (and *only* in Luke's Gospel) Jesus' *first* public act is a sort of "manifesto", a dramatic enactment and pronouncement, in synthesis, of the experience of Jesus through the whole of the Gospel. It takes place in the synagogue at Nazareth, where Jesus proclaims, through a reading of the Old Testament, that he is the fulfillment of the messianic expectations of Israel. It is important to see just which messianic texts from the Old Testament are used. Quoting from Is. 61,1-2 and Zeph. 2,3 Jesus announces:

> He has anointed me to preach good news to the poor.
> He has sent me to proclaim release to the captives
> and recovery of sight to the blind,
> to set at liberty those who are oppressed (Lk. 4,18).

Jesus claims that he is the anointed one of God, the Messiah, who has come — not to bless poverty, hunger and tears —but to release people from such sufferings.

If that is the case, what are we to make of the promise of the Lucan beatitudes? Precisely because they are poor, hungry and in tears, the Messiah will release them. Do they have any special privileges? Indeed they do. What is needed for the salvation which Jesus came to bring is a complete and radical openness to the word, person and life-style of Jesus of Nazareth. Here it is that the poor, the hungry and the afflicted are blessed. They have an advantage, as they are the ones who will welcome him. They are the people who will gladly welcome the Kingdom announced by Jesus, because they have no reason to defend the *status quo*. They will not set up a stern defence against the searing, questioning words of Jesus in protection of their own securities and interests . . . because they have no such interests! They are not happy with the *status quo*, and thus they make ideal men and women of faith. They possess that basic discontent with the present situation which is a basic pre-requisite for true faith. This must not be misunderstood. Their poverty is blessed because in their openness to an entirely new way, based on faith in all that Jesus has come to bring, they will be *liberated* from such a situation. The "woes" (Lk. 6,24-26) point in the other direction. There are many who have settled for the "here and now". Without a discontent with the *status quo* we settle for our "heaven on earth", and we have no openness to the new and perfect future which only God can create. The Christian faith is essentially a commitment to a journey, a "walking behind" Jesus of Nazareth (see, for example, Mark 1,16-20), as he leads us further and further away from ourselves into the mystery of an Exodus God. True Christian faith can never be a sitting down to be comfortable and happy with what we have under our control.

What is blessed in the Lucan beatitudes is not material poverty, despite the use made of Lk. 6,20b-22 by some contemporary writers. The poor, the hungry and the afflicted are blessed because they possess that one true possession: a radical openness to a new future which is the characteristic of a life of faith, and a very real possibility for the economically underprivileged. It must be stressed, however, that a material "having nothing" is never a biblical virtue in itself. It is blessed because, in Luke as in the experience of the Old Testament *anawim*, it can create an openness which is the ultimate source of all true blessings: an openness to God's future.

We should be warned against an automatic linking of material poverty with the Kingdom of God by the third and fourth beatitudes:

> Blessed are you that weep now, for you shall laugh. Blessed are you when men hate you, and when they exclude you and revile you, and cast out your name, on account of the Son of man! (Lk. 6,21-22).

It is not only the poor who weep; it is not only the poor who have been reviled and cast out because of their unflagging faith in the promise and in the person of Jesus of Nazareth. Yet, those who weep and those who are reviled are also promised the joys of the Kingdom. They too are always open to a new possibility. This is not to theorise, as we all know of the tragedies and anguish which, more often than not, seem to strike the lives of the wealthy . . . not to speak of the sufferings, still all too common in our own era, which cost the lives of believers, no matter what their financial situations, in the face of our modern, more sophisticated means of persecution. My confrere from Latin America has already spoken eloquently on such matters. Into these situations breaks an extraordinary possibility for faith. In the midst of tears and suffering, the wealthy and the rejeted are forced to their knees as they see that no one can control the ultimate hopes, plans and longings of mankind by means of purse strings or influential contacts. All of this is vain.

I hope that the reader is aware that I am not trying to "spiritualise" the message. The Lucan notion of poverty and suffering is very real, and was certainly based in the lived experience of such things. The Lucan beatitudes *do* speak to the economically poor and those in concrete situations of suffering. As Leonardo Boff has so rightly insisted:

> The messianic king will secure justice for the poor in the face of their oppressor. The magnanimity of the king extends to all. This Good News is for all the poor: the day of justice has come. The injustice of wealth and oppression will be revealed; this will in turn reveal the injustice

> of poverty. The Messiah upholds the right of the weak against the strong and the oppressor. 'Theirs is the Kingdom of Heaven' means that the poor will be the principal beneficiaries of the inbreaking of God's Kingdom, which is a new order of justice and equality and the overcoming of the distinction between rich and poor (L. Boff, *God's Witnesses in the Heart of the World*, p. 106).

Nevertheless, *in itself*, the possession of material goods is not an obstacle to evangelical poverty, nor to the possession of the Kingdom of God. In many cases it may prove to be so, because it is wealth which is the cause of poverty. In those cases, material possessions become evil. What must be seen, however, is that the Lucan beatitudes offer no biblical grounds for the all too common link which is made between material poverty and the following of Jesus. To be a follower of Jesus one does *not* have to renounce the dignity of possession and the joys of life; one does not have to live in abject poverty. The contrary, however, is still maintained, largely because of the story of the rich young man:

> Go, sell what you have and give to the poor (Mark 10,21). This seems to deny everything that we have said so far, and thus merits our particular attention.

The Story of the Rich Young Man

It may have come as somewhat of a surprise to many readers that there were two quite different versions of the beatitudes, in Matthew and Luke. The case is complicated even further with the so-called story of the rich young man. This story is found in each of the Synoptic Gospels: Mark 10,17-22, Matt. 19,16-22 and Luke 18,18-23. As we will see, there are basically only two versions, as Luke follows the Marcan account very closely, while Matthew seems to have rewritten his source (Mark) with a certain amount of freedom. However, rather than simply state these facts, I will again give each of the texts in a synoptic chart, so that the reader will be able to see the variations which have been introduced as the tradition has been taken and used by each evangelist.

Matt 19,16-22	*Mark 10,17-22*	*Luke 18,18-23*
16. And behold, one came up to him saying, "Teacher, what good deed must I do, to have eternal life?	17. And as he was setting out on his journey, a man ran up and knelt before him and asked him, "Good Teacher, what must I do to inherit eternal life?"	18. And a ruler asked him, Teacher, what shall I do to inherit eternal life?"
17. And he said to him, "Why do you ask me about what is good? One there is who is good. If you would enter life, keep the commandments." 18. He said to him, "Which?" And Jesus said, "You shall not commit adultery, You shall not steal, You shall not bear false witness, 19. Honour your father and mother, and, You shall love your neighbour as yourself".	18. And Jesus said to him, "Why do you call me good? No one is good but God alone. 19. You know the commandments: 'Do not commit adultery, Do not steal, Do not bear false witness, Do not defraud, Honour your father and mother'".	19. And Jesus said to him: Why do you call me good? No one is good but God alone. 20. You the commandments: 'Do not commit adultery, Do not kill, Do not bear false witness, Honour your father and mother'".
20. The young man said to him,	20. And he said to him, "Teacher,	21. And he said, "All these I have

"All these I have observed; what do I still lack?"	all these I have observed from my youth".	observed from my youth".
21. Jesus said to him, "If you would be perfect, go, sell what you possess and give to the poor, and you will have treasure in heaven; and come, follow me".	21. And Jesus looking upon him loved him, and said to him, "You lack one thing; go sell what you have, and give to the poor, and you will have treasure in heaven; and come, follow me".	22. And when Jesus heard it, he said to him, "One thing you still lack. Sell all that you have and distribute it to the poor, and you will have treasure in heaven and come, follow me".
22. When the young man heard this he went away sorrowful; for he had great possessions.	22. At that saying his countenance fell, and he went away sorrowful, for he had great possessions.	23. But when he heard this he became sad, for he was very rich.

If you have read through the parallels carefully, you will have noticed that Luke and Mark are very close. The main changes which have been made by Luke who, like Matthew, is using Mark's account as his source, have been his identification of Mark's "a man" (Mk. 10,17) as "a ruler" (Lk. 18,18), his reordering of the commandments (v. 20) and several stylistic changes, where Luke obviously felt that Mark's Greek needed some improving. An interesting detail which arises from a reading of *only* Mark and Luke is that we hear nothing of "a rich young man". That term is found only in the Matthean version. Matthew, although he is also using Mark as his source, has rewritten the story considerably. He has probably made the man into a rich young man through a reinterpretation of Mark 10,20: "Teacher, all these I have observed from my youth" into "The young man said to him, 'All these I have observed' " (Matt. 19,20). This detail — insignificant enough in itself — assumes a certain importance when we consider that the story is known to us all as "The Story of the Rich Young Man". Over the centuries, the version which has always been most widely used in the Liturgy and in exhortations to Religious has been the Matthean version. Thus, to most Christians, it is indeed "the story of the rich young man" which is widely known and cited. However, I would like to offer a short analysis of the Marcan story, which really stands at the beginning of the tradition. I will make some further remarks on the Mathean rewriting of the story at a later stage. It has been so important in our tradition that it merits our particular attention.

The Marcan version, used as a source by both Matthew and Luke, begins with a very difficult question and answer which need not delay us. The man, in requesting the way to inherit eternal life, addresses Jesus as "Good Teacher" (Mk. 10,17). Jesus' answer, that only God is good (v. 18) has implications about the relative goodness of Jesus himself. Notice that while Luke is prepared to leave this ambiguity, as he simply repeats Mark, Matthew tries to avoid it by remodelling the whole discussion:

> Rich man: "Teacher, what good deed must I do?"
> Jesus: "Why do you ask me what is good?" (Matt. 19,16-17)

Having settled that only God is good, Jesus tests the justice of the man, according to the Law of Israel. This is the pont of the list of commandments which Jesus asks him to observe (Mk. 10,19). Jesus does not give a list of all the commandments. Those chosen are what we might call the social commandments, those which deal with his treatment of his neighbour: adultery, theft, false witness, defrauding and respect for parents. These are the commandments which a powerful, rich man would be most prone to offend.

It is easy enough to observe (at least externally) one's ritual obligations towards God and Church while dealing unjustly and sinfully with one's weaker neighbour. Again, we do not have to look far in our contemporary world for examples of well-decorated, uniformed heads of state photographed beside Cardinal Primates on the steps of many Latin American cathedrals. The point needs no further elaboration. Luke has made this very point very well by simply changing Mark's vague reference to the hero of the story as "a man" to "a ruler" (Lk. 18,18).

The man replies that he has lived a life of love and respect for his neighbour all his life. On hearing this reply , "Jesus looking upon him loved him" (Mk. 10,21). Notice that this is the first indication of a movement from Jesus towards the man. So far all the initiative has come from the man himself. Quite capable of doing everything that he sets out to do, and having the means to do it, he asks Jesus' advice on the attainment of eternal life. Jesus now sees that the man has a deep desire to go further than he has gone so far through his observance of the commandments, and so, loving him, he attempts to wrest the initiative from the man, and he then calls him to discipleship:

> You lack one thing; go sell what you have and give to the poor, and you will have treasure in heaven; and come, follow me (Mk. 10,21).

This is the radical demand which has inspired many generous and courageous hearts to extraordinary initiatives, but these wonderful examples from the history of Christian life must not be allowed to lead us astray in our attempt to rediscover the real point of this famous story. The use of the technical term: "Come, follow me", links this account to a series of other vocation stories in Mark's Gospel, especially 1,16-20; 2,13-17 and 3,13-19. In each of those stories one of the outstanding features of the vocation to discipleship was the *absolute initiative* of Jesus, and the immediate, wordless obedience of the one called. We have already seen that here the initiative has come from the rich man. In comparison with the other Marcan vocation stories, another feature emerges. Even though the first disciples leave their nets, boats, hired servants and their father (1,16-20) and Levi leaves his tax-house (2,13-15), there is no command that they should sell everything and give it to the poor before they could hope to become disciples of Jesus. Such a command is found *only* in this story. In fact, if there is any historical background to John 21, the disciples returned to the lake and their fishing after the paschal events.

Two problems are emerging. Why is this man (and no other disciple) asked to sell everything and give it to the poor before he can follow Jesus? Is it a universal law of the Gospel that *only* those who follow such a course of action can regard themselves as disciples of Jesus? The solution to the first problem, in fact, will make sense or non-sense of the second. We must look closely at the text itself. The key to the whole passage is found in the self-confident request of the rich man, found in all three versions of the account (Mk. 10,17; Matt. 19,16; Lk. 18,18): "What must *I do* to inherit eternal life?" Here we have a man who is used to deciding his own destiny, because he has the power and the wealth to force the issue. As we have just seen in our analysis of the Lucan beatitudes, this is not the way of faith. To become a disciple of Jesus, *this man* has to be stripped of all that stands between him and a radical commitment to Jesus. *In the case of this man*, it is his wealth. He is blocked from a total commitment to Jesus because he wants to control his own destiny, as he always has. Even in his enquiries about the best way to come to eternal life, he is simply asking what *he* must do. Thus, the means he has at his disposal to dictate such terms must go. The story is ultimately about the radical nature of true faith. One must have sufficient trust and faith in the person of Jesus of Nazareth to be able to pay the price ... and it costs no less than everything. All that stands between the believer and an unconditional surrender of self to Jesus must be stripped away, but this man fails, and sorrowfully loses his chance of discipleship (v. 22).

There is another potential disciple of Jesus in the Marcan

Gospel who tries to take the initiative. After the Gerasene demoniac has been cured, he "begged him (Jesus) that he might be with him" (5,18). Exactly parallel with our story, Jesus wrests the initiative from him:

> But he refused, and said to him, "Go home to your friends, and tell them how much the Lord has done for you, and how he has had mercy on you" (5,19).

In contrast to the reaction of our rich man, the Gerasene demoniac responds in wordless obedience, and becomes the first Gentile missionary:

> And he went away and began to proclaim in the Decapolis how much Jesus had done for him; and all men marveled (5,20)

In the case of the ex-demoniac, all earlier pretensions fall away, and he obediently and joyfully goes off on his mission (5,20), but the contrary is the case with the rich man, and he "went away sorrowful", a lost vocation to discipleship (10,22).

This lengthy analysis should show that our story is *not* a universal call to all who would wish to become disciples of Jesus to reduce themselves to a state of financial indigence. That is to universalise the wrong problem. The question of possessions was the one thing lacking *for that man.* It was the final hindrance between the rich man and his radical commitment to Jesus as his disciple. It is from here that we must draw conclusions about the universal application of the story. What is of universal significance is the need to shed all pretensions to power, to shake off the desire to dictate terms in the Kingdom, to be rid of anything which stands between ourselves and a radical *following* (never leading) of Jesus of Nazareth.

There is a similar story, with the same call to radical faith, in Matt. 8,21-22. Within a context dealing with discipleship (see vv. 18-27) we find the following:

> Another of the disciples said to him, "Lord, let me first go and bury my father". But Jesus said to him, "Follow me, and leave the dead to bury their own dead".

Thank goodness we have had the common sense not to universalise the wrong details of that particular story! As with the rich man, between this disciple and Jesus there stands an obstacle. However, in this case it is not possessions and power, but an affective relationship. It must go! As can be clearly seen, both stories concern themselves with the radical nature of true faith. To be a disciple of Jesus means that one must be prepared to pay any price, in order to "follow" him. Wealth and affective relationships can block our commitment to Jesus, but these accounts must never be taken as a Gospel message that *only* those who are economically underprivileged, and *only* those without attachments to their families, their father, mother, wife, husband and children, can become disciples of Jesus. That would make the Gospel message quite irrelevant to the major part of Christianity — not to speak of humanity — and to make a lie out of our own experience. It has probably been the genuine faith and genuine evangelical poverty which we have experienced within the context of our own families that we have learnt most about the following of Jesus of Nazareth.

I indicated earlier that Matthew's version of the story of the rich young man has played a large part in the formation of our traditional ideas on poverty, and especially on the vow of poverty, taken by the Religious. As Matthew rewrote his source (Mark 10,16-22) his major contribution was that the rich young man could become "perfect" if he sold his possessions, gave to the poor, and followed Jesus (Matt. 19,21). This has long been read as an indication that there was a superior state among Christians. If you merely want to have "eternal life", then all you need do is live by the commandments (19,17-19), but if you want to be "perfect", then you must embrace the voluntary, evangelical *counsel* of poverty (vv. 20-21). Of course, this theology of "perfection" is found only in Matthew's version of the story. Again I must insist that we will only be able to come to a correct understanding of the passage if we are prepared to situate it within Matthew's Gospel as a whole. This Gospel was written for a community of largely ex-Jewish Christians. One of the difficulties faced by this community was their relationship to the old Law. Israel had lived faithful to that Law for almost two thousand years and now Matthew's community was wondering just how they were to relate to it, as disciples of Jesus. The question is dealt with pretty extensively in Matt. 5.

The major part of Matt. 5 shows Jesus, the new lawgiver, presenting his Law, over against the Law of Moses. Six times he actually cites the old Law to his audience, introducing it with the phrase used by the Rabbis to quote from the Law: "You have heard that it was said to the men of old . . . " (v. 21), and similar fixed phrases (see vv. 27, 31, 33, 38, 43). Each time he quotes from the Torah itself, but then concludes: "But I say to you . . . " (see vv. 22, 28, 32, 34, 39, 44). Jesus does not deny the Law, but he internalises it, asking his followers to realise that they must commit themselves to a fulness of the Law which must strike at the very depths of their existence. This long passage throughout Matt. 5 is but an exemplification of a principle which Jesus himself had stated in 5,17: "Think not that I have come to abolish the law and the prophets; I have come not to abolish them but to fulfill them" (see also vv. 18-20). In this way, Jesus answers the problems of the Matthean community: they are no longer called to observe the detailed *precepts* so jealously guarded by first century Judaism; they are called to the fulfillment of the law, to a perfection and a fulness which only Jesus could offer. At the end of the discourse of Matt. 5 the radical nature of the new life of "higher righteousness" to which the Christian is called is made strikingly clear:

> You therefore must be *perfect*, as your heavenly Father is *perfect* (5,48).

This remarkable imperative, with its two-fold use of the word "perfect", takes us directly to 19,16-22, where the rich young man was also called to be "perfect". In the whole of the Gospel of Matthew, this term is found only in 5,48 and 19,21.

I would now like to point out the profound parallel which exists between Matt. 5 and 19,16-22. We have just seen that the context of the first of the "perfection" sayings from Jesus (Matt. 5) is a carefully written presentation of the Law of Jesus over against the Law of Moses, in which the old Law is shown to be brought to its fulfilment, to its perfection, in Jesus of Nazareth. The Christian life, therefore, is intimately tied up with the radical new righteousness which results from a living of Jesus' new Law. The whole discussion is concluded by a call to "perfection" (5,48). *Exactly* the same argument is being pursued through the narrative of the rich young man. The rich young man has lived a life which has been according to the *precepts* of the old Law (19,18-20). He is able to say, honestly, that as far as the Law of Moses is concerned, "All these I have observed" (v. 20). Jesus, in the light of this fact, then calls him to be his disciple, to become a Christian. The term used here (v.21), as in 5,48, to speak of the vocation to the Christian life is: "If you will be *perfect*". As in Mark's Gospel, the condition which is demanded from the rich young man is that he sell his goods and give to the poor. At this stage of the account, Matthew is repeating Mark's insistence that the vocation to Christian life will cost the young man no less than everything. As in Mark 10,17-22, Matthew 19,16-22 is primarily a message about the radical nature of the faith required from anyone who wishes to embrace the "perfection" which is to be found uniquely in the following of Jesus. It is to do violence to Matthew's message to find here a biblical proof for a distinction between "ordinary" Christians, following the commandments, and "vowed" Christians, living according to evangelical counsels. The rich young man was not called to the Religious life — but to Christian life, and Matthew calls that life, in both 5,48 and 19,21, a life of perfection.

Nevertheless, somehow these traditionally used Gospel passages do apply to our lives of evangelical poverty. We have seen from our analysis of the passages from Paul and from the Acts of the Apostles that our poverty is never an end in itself. It must be an expression of a deeper reality: the profound desire to share all that we have and all that we are because we have been united into a unique bond of love through the remarkable gift of our faith in Christ Jesus. This radical sharing — the true sense of evangelical poverty —announces to the world, not the evil of possessions, but the value of a shared life inspired by an unconditional response to the radical life of faith demanded from the rich young man. Our poverty, therefore, announces to the world that faith in Jesus makes us "different". Our shared lives of faith and love are outwardly reflected in the sharing of all that we are and all that we have, and it must make the world stop and wonder what makes us live this way. Our answer to a questioning, critical world must not be phrased in terms of economics or sacrifice, but in terms of that extraordinary gift which is ours: a new life of faith which is "life in Christ".

A Shared Responsibility for the Life of the Community

All that we have seen so far is not exclusive to the Religious life. In fact, some Religious may feel that I am depriving them of the aspects of their commitment which they felt were unique to their form of life. My examination of the biblical material nevertheless, has made it clear that, in one form or another, evangelical poverty, which is one of the external consequences of our life in Christ, is a part of the vocation to "perfection" of all the baptised (see *Lumen Gentium*, 40). This final section should also be seen in the same fashion, but as I will now be looking into more practical questions, I will have to limit myself to the way in which this New Testament notion of a shared life works itself out in the practice of a vowed community in such a way that it proclaims to the world what "life in Christ" can really mean.

Still, *mutatis mutandis*, there is nothing in the reflections which follow which could not be applied to any Christian. This is the case because, even though I will necessarily concentrate my attention upon the ideal of the Religious community, all Christians, in some form or other, live community.

It stands to reason that no community, whether Religious or not, can survive unless each one of the members of that community is prepared to assume an *active* responsibility for the other members. If our Christian existence depends upon our readiness to share at all levels, in the simplest and in the deepest of our affairs, then all of us must be productive. Primarily, each one of us must generate the faith, the hope and the love which sustains others. Religious should be much more conscious of the innumerable examples of this form of sharing which can be found in almost every Religious community: the smiling face and the deep calm of the infirm or elderly confrere which makes the struggling youngster aware that this form of life produces great human beings, the daily commitment to long hours and difficult tasks, which many are not really equipped to handle, the genuine love and loss of self among those who live side by side with difficult and sick people. The list could go on much further, but these few examples will have to suffice. Far too often Religious fail to see the enormous witness value of such a genuine sharing of life. It is merely accepted as part and parcel of our lot. It is much more! When "poverty" is properly understood as a sharing of all that we are and all that we have, as a genuine expression of the oneness of life which is created by our faith, then the sharing which I have just described must be understood as a vital part of lives publicly vowed to poverty. I want to insist on the *primary* importance of this aspect of the sharing of life that goes on in all Religious communities, because the rest of these more practical applications will be devoted to more material questions. They are tremendously important — but they would be senseless unless this primary function of a vow of poverty is being lived. Although this aspect of poverty is grossly undervalued by most Religious, it is an aspect of their lives which must be seen and understood by the Church and the world in which they live and for which they exist. The self-sacrificing sharing at a very deep level which is a central aspect of a successful Religious community has enormous witness potential, but traditionally we have hesitated to allow people to see it, or even hear about it. We have built high walls around our monasteries and our convents and we have placed severe restrictions upon just who could share our table and our life. Although a great deal has been done to remedy this situation, still more has to be done. We need not fear our weaknesses and our tensions, as it is precisely here that the world will see that such problems need not destroy a community which is seriously committed to "life in Christ".

Having made that point, I must now insist that a similar productivity is also required at the level of material goods. This is where the notion of poverty as "having nothing" falls short of the Christian ideal. There is no one — no matter how aged, infirm or incompetent — who has nothing. Each one of us is a unique creation of God, and this necessarily flows into what each one of us does, as we reach out to serve or love the other. It is most unfortunate, but one of the subtlest surrenders to the absolutes which culture and secular society live by is found precisely here. Too often there is too much time and effort given to the perfection of one's "gifts". However, not all are "gifted", in the narrow sense that secular culture gives to that term. Yet, once we look at people and life with the eyes of faith, then all are "gifted", and this giftedness will be reflected in what we are to people and what we do for them, no matter how modest that may be.

The idea that poverty is to have nothing and to wait for God to send bread from heaven has been seen as what the Gospels demand. I hope that my lengthy and detailed examination of the New Testament evidence, using the skills which contemporary scholarship has given me, has shown that this is to misunderstand the Gospels. My conclusions are borne out in practice, as very often such an attitude can lead to a bone-lazy materialism and a living off the goods which are earned by the hard work of the *other* members of the community, or, worse still, a living off the charity of an adoring laity which considers itself as second class, and which subconsciously feels that some holiness will rub off if they associate with the priests, the brothers, or the "poor sisters". A part of the essential vocation of men and women is a vocation to work (see Gen. 1,26-31; 3,7-19), and no Religious is called to live off his or her local community.

A look at the history of the Religious life shows that from the earliest days communities have seen it as their responsibility to work hard to provide for their own needs. Pachomius, the founder of the cenobitic life (circa 290-346), hired himself and his monks out to work in the fields during the harvest season and Basil the Great (circa 330-379) demanded that all his monks have a trade. The great father of western monasticism, St. Benedict (circa 480-550) coined the significant motto for his monks: "Ora et labora" — Pray and work. The name that comes to mind immediately, as an objection to my argument, is that of St. Francis of Assisi (1181-1226), so often romanticised in this connection. In fact, he was proud to earn his living, and he ordered his followers to continue working at the trades which they had practised before they had joined him. It is also important to know that he permitted his followers to beg only when there was no work, or when the salary was not enough to live on (*Regula Prima*, 7; Test., 19-22)

The place where Religious are most clearly seen in action is at their work. As this is the case it is within the sphere of each particular apostolic activity that they must raise serious questions, and not just "do a job". As this is the case, the poverty of the Religious must also be seen as they are at work. This must not be misunderstood. Our poverty does not begin and end with our work. My insistence upon the *primary* function of the sharing of life within community should have made that clear. We do not exist so that we might work. On the contrary, the work which the Religious does in the Church and world must raise questions: why do talented, professional and hard-working (or maybe, not so talented, not so professional and not so hard-working) people work and live together . . . in that particular house, in that particular street? It should be made clear that they do *not* work for their own self-aggrandisement, for their professional advancement. The work of the Religious is not done to further a career, primarily. Why, then, does this community exist? The answer must be because they have come together in faith and love, to follow the way of Jesus of Nazareth. The witness value of our poverty does not lie in our parading through the streets with the soles of our shoes flapping off or our elbows showing through our jackets. That sort of thing may raise eyebrows, but it does not command respect. If our lives of poverty are going to be an evangelising force, then they must create admiration, and a desire to somehow be caught up in the same love and unity which makes the Religious live in this way. Our poverty calls us to a radical sharing of all that we are and all that we have, so that we may produce a quality of community life that makes people stop and wonder. When the world sees that all our efforts are directed, not to personal aggrandisement, but to the support and strengthening of our life in Christ, then we may be seen as "world stoppers", questioning the futile values that the world creates when it makes a god of personal success and material values.

Evangelical poverty must never be reduced to a means by which those who dedicate themselves to the Religious life are freed from financial worries, so that they may work and pray more effectively. As we have seen through our analysis of the biblical background to this all-important Christian commitment, we are moving in the mysterious area of faith in Christ. Evangelical poverty is an inescapable consequence which flows from the unity of love created by such a faith (see, again, Acts 2,44-45 and 4,32-35). As this is the case, our commitment to evangelical poverty can show to the world that Christians share all that they have and all that they are, because they share "life in Christ". In a discussion of the vow of poverty, obviously its practice must be worked out within the area of material things. In a Religious community the practice of evangelical poverty could perhaps be formulated in the following fashion: all that I have I give *to* the community, and all that I need I receive *from* the community. This practice, however, must flow from a deeper reality, which again may be formulated simply: all that I am I give *to* the community, and in my need for encouragement, support, guidance and friendship, I turn confidently to my community, knowing that it will come *from* there. Living in this way, each member of the community knows and experiences that the responsibility for the material well-being of the community — at all levels — lies with all the members of the community, and not only with those whose task it is to keep the books and sign the cheques! However, as should be more than obvious by now, the sharing of responsibility at a material level is *nothing*, if it is not an external sign of a deeper reality: the extraordinary preparedness to lose oneself in love and service, in imitation of Jesus of Nazareth, which must be the heart and soul of the spirituality of every Christian and every Christian community.

Conclusion

All Christians are called by the Gospels to a radical sharing of all that they have and all that they are and hope to be. I hope that my analysis of the material from the New Testament has shown this to be the case. The message of the Gospel is clear: all men should have the possibility of becoming all that God made them to be. To make this possible, the Gospel ideal is that all peoples are called to a radical sharing. This, ultimately, was the sense of Luke's ideal presentation of the Church in his portrait of the apostolic community in the Acts of the Apostles: "There was not a needy person among them" (Acts 4,34).

Such a model, nevertheless, remains an ideal, and the signs of our times indicate that the world — and possibly the Christian Church itself — does not seem to be coming to grips with these Gospel values. We see a Christian Europe and a Christian North America living with an easy conscience beside Africa and Latin America. But these are the immediately obvious examples of the scandal of contemporary Christian society. Closer to home, in each city, village and hamlet, society is clearly divided along the lines which have been drawn between those who have and those who do not have. What is worse, such a situation is never questioned, and western society uses possessions to judge the success or failure of any particular individual or society. As society spirals towards a disastrous situation of millions of unemployed and management locks itself in bitter struggle against a turbulent, protesting work force, we seem to be almost on the threshold of some sort of apocalyptic moment. In all of this turmoil, however, it never seems to strike anyone that all this strife is nothing more — nor less — than a subconscious screaming out that men and women were not made to live in this way. We live in a world so tragically marked by a breakdown of care for the other that Jean Paul Sartre could claim that "hell is other people" and a popular song can proclaim "hell is in hello". As I type these pages we raise our eyebrows slightly when we hear of the rape and murder of a six year old girl in a suburb around the corner. The spirit of the age seems to be that the only way to pleasure, happiness, success and survival is to grab what you can while the going is good.

Although not marked by the same sort of public violence, there are deep divisions between the "haves" and the "have-nots" within the confines of the confessing Christian Churches. Very often wealth of possessions and culture in one community can peacefully go on existing beside terrible poverty — at all levels — in another. The people "looking in", those outside the confessing Churches, are quick to see the lie. Unlike the non-Christians' witness to the life of the earliest Church, our contemporaries are able to point out that while the Church *preaches* the Gospel of Jesus Christ, it *lives* according to the gospel of secular culture.

Within this situation, the public commitment of a Religious community to evangelical poverty, the radical sharing of all that it has and all that it is, takes on a prophetic function in both the world and the Church. The members of a Religious community have publicly vowed themselves to a showing to the world, by the quality of their shared life, that true humanity — and thus true Christianity — is not just a *preached* message. Despite the many critical situations which arise both within and from outside the Church, Religious are able to show that the reality of evangelical poverty is a *lived* reality — within the Church. The vow of poverty for a Religious is not an end in itself. It is an all-important means to an end: it is a major aspect of the prophetic function of the Religious within the Church, showing the Church and the world that it is only through the freedom won by a radical observance of evangelical poverty that we can ever hope to love as Christ loved.

We must try to avoid the hard and fast definitions of the *things* which make for poverty. This will necessarily vary. It should be a matter of plain common sense that the material context of no two communities (even in the same city) can ever be exactly the same. There can be no universal list of what we can have or not have. What is of paramount importance, however, is that our disdain for the slavery of the world to personal achievements, possessions and aggrandisement on the material plane be *visible*. This necessarily puts us within the context of material things, and the vow of poverty must be worked out there. Nevertheless, they must not be the ultimate measure of our poverty — our shared life "in Christ" is. We cannot confine this to intellectual and practical criteria. Subtly, to allow the lists of "haves" and "have-nots" is to submit, like the rest of society which we are trying to question, to the criterion of materialism itself. The roots of our poverty cannot and must not be intellectualised, because the reciprocal dependence and productivity, at all levels, which are the essence of the vow to evangelical poverty, cannot be intellectualised and made into a list of "things". It acquires its value only if it is motivated by love of an exceptional quality.

Reasons can always be found for lists of "do's and don'ts" or "may-haves" and "may-not-haves", but if we are honest, we must admit that the need for such lists in our communities reflects a rather painful truth: the reality of our lives together, the quality of our shared "life in Christ" is often very poor. Given that situation, we rush to create structures, to draw up lists, which will convey (primarily to ourselves, as others are generally not fooled) an impression that we are "poor". The immediate practical problem with this system, however, is that the self-centred, non-sharing member of a community can be perfect in matters of "poverty" (?), while every vestige of a truly biblically based and evangelical poverty has been lost, as the community divides . . . generally in anger around the selfishness of that very person.

Genuine love, the self-sacrificing love of Christ, cannot be measured by laws and lists, as it goes beyond any sort of material measurement. Our vow of poverty is one of our major means of showing to the world that we are committed to this love, and that we are summoning all who live by the Gospel to see the urgency of the biblical imperative of evangelical poverty in the lives of all Christians. When we examine our consciences on poverty we must, therefore, begin with a serious look at the level of our shared lives of love. Only when we have come to grips with this basic motive for our very existence as a Christian community should we turn our attention to the material circumstances of our lives, as they are only the context within which our poverty, our shared life "in Christ", must work itself out.

CHASTITY

While the urgency of contemporary economic problems and the obvious use and abuse of power and possessions going on around us can lead us quickly to see the universal value of a life committed to evangelical poverty, a commitment to chastity, as it is often understood, could still appear to be pointless. Perhaps it could be justly said that we are living in the midst of a crisis of chastity. By that statement I do not simply mean that Priests and Religious are critical of the celibate state, and many appear to be quite disenchanted by such a form of life. That is only a minor aspect of a much wider phenomenon, where marriage is falling apart as an institution and a healthy appreciation of one's own sexuality and the sexuality of others is something of an exception. That may be a slight overstatement of the case, but I am sure that the reader will grant that something is seriously wrong with the Western world's use and abuse of the treasure of sexuality. We cannot hope to analyse this phenomenon in these pages, but it is the context within which we must attempt to understand the evangelical imperative of chastity.

It appears to me that a false step has been taken in recent years among Religious in the identification of "chastity" with "celibacy". There has been an unfortunate tendency among some contemporary writers on the Religious life and the vows to single out the uniqueness of the celibate state of the Religious, and to argue that it is the distinguishing mark of the Religious state within the context of the universal call to holiness in the Church. In fact, several authors and indeed several congregations in their post-Vatican II constitutions have moved away from the traditional terms: poverty, chastity and obedience, to speak of celibacy, poverty and obedience. I am not concerned with the change in order. That is irrelevant. However, it is far from unimportant to shift from "chastity" to "celibacy" as a term for the vow taken by the Religious. We must recognise that we stand at the end of 1,600 years of tradition, where this aspect of the vowed life has always been called "chastity". If such is the case, then it is reasonable to think that there must be very good reasons for the use of such a term. It appears to me that the reason is near at hand. I am insisting, throughout this book, that we should not speak of evangelical counsels, but of evangelical imperatives, aimed at all who are committed to the following of Jesus of Nazareth. Although not immediately obvious, it can be shown, easily enough, that all committed Christians attempt to live lives marked by evangelical poverty and evangelical obedience in some form. It is also extremely important for us to understand that all Christians, celibate or married, are called to chastity. In fact, most Christians live a vowed form of chastity. Some of us publicly profess this vow and commit ourselves to a Religious community, where we attempt to live out the high ideals of a celibate form of chastity. Others publicly profess it in the marriage ceremony and commit themselves to a husband or wife in the *equally demanding ideal* of the chastity found in faithful and fruitful conjugal love.

While what follows will be largely concerned with the theology and the practice of the celibate form of chastity, I hope that the reader will sense throughout my analysis of the conciliar and biblical material that what the Gospels say about celibate love applies powerfully to conjugal love. For too long these two forms of the same commitment to evangelical chastity have been seen in a contrasting fashion, as far too much stress has been given to the presence or absence of physical love-making within the two life-styles.

There needs to be greater clarity over the meaning of the words "celibate" and "chaste". The former is a word used to speak of an unmarried person, who does not have a regular and established sexual relationship with a husband or a wife (*The Shorter Oxford English Dictionary:* "unmarried, single, bound not to marry"). The latter word says nothing about one's sexual situation in life. Chastity refers to the *manner in which* one lives one's sexuality. A chaste person is one who has a healthy, holy, loving and God-directed attitude to the gift of his own and others' sexuality. It indicates a person whose sexual life is blameless, be he or she married or celibate (*The Shorter Oxford English Dictionary:* "pure from unlawful sexual intercourse, continent, virtuous"). Thus, "celibacy" is a physical state; it is not, in itself, a Christian virtue. One can only speak of virtue when one refers to "chastity".

This may appear to be hair-splitting, but the confusion at the level of language which we have seen is a reflection of a deeper problem. The tendency of some authors to argue that the distinguishing mark of the Religious in the Church is consecrated celibacy is well-intentioned and, in many ways, well-founded. It is certainly one of the most prophetic gestures of the Religious life in contemporary society. Nevertheless, we must resist the tendency to argue that the Religious is "vowed to celibacy". Such an expression is so common today that my claim could even appear outrageous. I do not wish to be misunderstood, but a consideration of just what "celibacy" means would show that one's being "vowed to celibacy" means that one is vowed to a physical state, that the essence of the vow is not to have a wife or a husband with whom one has a stable sexual relationship. This is certainly true of the vowed life as we attempt to live it, but it must be seen and understood as a *consequence* of one's vow to live chastely. To be vowed to celibacy is not a virtue in itself. A virtuous sexual life is called "chaste", and does not necessarily involve celibacy. I hope that I am not labouring the point too much, but it is very important that we retain our traditional terminology: there are a great number of celibates who are not particularly chaste, while there are many non-celibates whose chastity is outstanding.

There are various consequences which flow from these important considerations, but I can only mention a few of them, in passing.

a) Theologically, the vowed life must be based on Gospel values. Christians are not called to any particular physical state. As I hope to show, there is no solid biblical support for the idea that any particular *physical* state is essential for virtue. That sort of dangerous heresy did raise its voice in the early centuries of the Church's history, but was eventually defeated as the Church's thought evolved. Christians are free to marry or to commit themselves to virginity, and to live the *virtue* of chastity in whatever way of life they choose. In this way we can speak of the evangelical imperative of chastity, a universal vocation to a wholeness of life and love. Some will be married, some will be celibate, but all are summoned by the Gospels to follow the chaste Jesus of Nazareth.

b) Pastorally, the claim that celibacy is the essence of a vow makes for all sorts of difficulties. Serious sin, and for some more delicate people, even difficulties of a non-sinful nature in the affective and sexual area would indicate that the vow has been broken. If one's Christian life is judged according to one's measurable success or failure in matters physical, then success in the Christian life has been cheapened. The vows of poverty and obedience are virtues towards which we strive all our lives. A "vow of celibacy" allows for no such dynamism and historical growth in grace and virtue. If the measure of one's virtue is one's physical state, then a person in difficulty will soon despair. However, if we retain the traditional term "chastity", then egoism, failure and real sinfulness along the journey to perfect chastity can be recognised as such, pardon can be sought, and a person's life can be reconstructed as he or she picks up the pieces and strives to live the vow and virtue of chastity. We all have difficulties with poverty and obedience. Most of us are prepared to admit such weaknesses, but we struggle all our lives with them. They seldom lead us into despair. So must it also be with the vow of chastity.

The Objections to Chaste Celibacy

We are all well aware of the series of objections that are put to a life of chastity, under any form, from the secularised world which uses sex to add colour and interest to even the most innocent human interests and pastimes. A few hours in front of a television set will teach us all we need to know about such objections. There is no point in my listing these objections, or lamenting them. Nevertheless, we must be aware of them, as it is to our heavily sexualised world that our chastity must speak. As with poverty, so the chastity of the Christian must *speak* to the sexual disorder which has always been part and parcel of man's sinful situation. We will never make any impact upon our world by talking about chastity unless behind the words there are lives which make people ask if, perhaps, they have not lost their way.

If such is the case with the universal call of all Christians to live their chastity, so must the Religious regard his or her particular form of chastity: celibacy. However, the Second Vatican Council spoke eloquently, for the first time in the Church's official teaching, of the salvific value of created things (see *Gaudium et Spes*, 33-39) and developed a powerfully biblical and contemporary theology of marriage (*Gaudium et Spes*, 47-52). Although these two aspects of the Church's teaching, presented in this way for the first time, come from their own theological background and have their own particular context within the overall argument of the Conciliar document on the Church in the Modern World, they have two further ramifications which are important for our considerations:

1. They have provided us with a positive and moving theology and practice of marriage, well-adapted to the needs and questions of our own era.

2. They seriously question some of the traditional motives for celibate chastity.

I must stress here, however, that these teachings did not simply fall out of the heavens as the Council was meeting. They were merely the final magisterial articulation of theological reflection which had been widely spread in the Catholic Church for the greater part of the century. The immediate influences were the seminal work of Teilhard de Chardin, and then the more properly theological work of such great figures as Yves Congar, Henri de Lubac and Karl Rahner.

As we have just seen, the first of these new teachings has concerned the salvific value of created reality. As a traditional spirituality attempted to show the superiority of the celibate state, there was a tendency to play down all that was "natural". This way of seeing things arose from a theology, and consequently a spirituality, which made a distinction between the natural and the supernatural. Man's being "supernatural" was seen as best expressed by his being virginal, as this lifted him out of the trammels of the flesh and the preoccupations of the married state, and all the "worldly" interests which are a necessary consequence of being married. This led to an under-valuation — and at times a rather negative view — of all that was natural and physical. It was this sort of theological background which produced the many pious reflections which spoke of the celibate state as being "angelic" and the better way, the more spiritual way. Purity was commonly referred to as "the angelic virtue". Striking at the very roots of such a position, catching up the work of the great pre-conciliar studies (especially those of Henri de Lubac) which showed that the well-worn distinction between nature and supernature was a false one, Vatican II devoted a chapter of its decree on the Church in the Modern World to a consideration of man's activity within the context of created reality (*Gaudium et Spes*, 33-39). The role of created reality in the plan of God was beautifully expressed as the Church proclaimed:

> If by the autonomy of earthly affairs is meant the gradual discovery, exploitation and ordering of the laws and values of matter and society, then the demand for autonomy is perfectly in order: *it is at once the claim of modern man and the desire of the creator*. By the very nature of creation, material being is endowed with its own stability, truth and excellence, its own order and laws ... Believers, no matter what their religion, have always recognised the voice and the revelation of God in the language of creatures. Besides, once God is forgotten, the creature is lost sight of as well (*Gaudium et Spes*, 36. Stress mine).

Men and women are not saved *despite* their belonging to the world of material things, *despite* the fact that they are flesh and blood, and therefore sexual beings, but *because of it*, and in and through their being situated in God's creation. We are all inextricably caught up in God's creative plan, and any theology of chastity — be it conjugal or celibate — must be worked out in this light.

Perfectly coherent with their own teaching on the salvific value of created reality, the Council Fathers went on to develop a splendid presentation of the sanctity of the married state, and the sanctification which comes to the married through a life of faithful gift of self in conjugal love. Here the teaching of the Church leans heavily on biblical concepts, and explicitly on Eph. 5,21-33:

> Just as of old God encountered his people with a covenant of love and fidelity, so our Saviour, the spouse of the Church, now encounters Christian spouses through the sacrament of marriage. He abides with them in order that by their mutual self-giving spouses will love each other with enduring fidelity, as he loved the Church and delivered himself for it. Authentic married love is caught up into divine love and is directed and enriched by the

> redemptive power of Christ and the salvific action of the Church (*Gaudium et Spes*, 48).

There are two very important points to be noted here. There is the wonderful parallel drawn between the gift of Jesus in his sacrifice of self for the Church, and the "mutual self-giving" of married couples. The Church has touched upon that very aspect of marriage which is so cheapened and debased by contemporary culture, and which has been somewhat frowned upon and considered as an unfortunate necessity in certain areas of Christian spirituality. By faithfully interpreting Eph. 5,21-33 she has shown that its closest parallel is to be found in the most wonderful moment in the history of God's relationship with mankind: Christ's gift of himself for us. Secondly, the Church has stated that, in a situation of "authentic married love", we have the revelation of God's love reflected in the redemptive power of Christ at work in their lives, as they are swept into the reality of divine love itself. There is no possibility — within the Christian view of things — that such a state in life could be considered "second-class" citizenship in the Kingdom. It is clearly a wonderfully privileged place among men and women where a God who is love is revealed, and where men and women can find an exquisite means of sanctification.

We are able to rise from our reading of the Church's teaching refreshed by this rich vision of the vow of chastity and the practice of conjugal love in marriage. However, there is another important area in the life of the Church where chastity is practised: in the celibate love of the person consecrated to that particular form of life. What is the place of the vow of chastity and the practice of celibate love in the Religious life?

The Traditional Case for Celibate Chastity

The Church has always seen virginity as having a special place among Christians. It appears that the saying from Jesus about being "eunuchs for the sake of the kingdom of heaven" in Matt. 19,12 is a Gospel passage which shows the superiority of virginity, and Paul certainly advised the Corinthians that if they were not married they would do well to remain so "to secure your undivided attention to the Lord" (see I Cor. 7,32-35). From there the early centuries of the Church saw a great concentration on the state of virginity. Nearly all the great Fathers of the Church devoted attention to the question, and most produced a "De Virginitate". In fact, the writings of the Fathers of the early Church reflect an underlying feeling that baptism and matrimony go together rather uncomfortably, ultimately turning to Paul's famous dictum: "It is better to marry than to be aflame with passion" (I Cor. 7,9). Perhaps one of the greatest of the Fathers, St. Augustine (354-430), is the best example for us to take. Attempting to explain, in his struggle against the Pelagians, that infants needed grace, he had to solve the problem of how an innocent child could be "of the world" and not "of Christ". One must remember that Augustine, and the other Fathers of the Church, had no well-established dogmas to work out of. These were the people who were forging what we have come to know as Christian theology. In this case, for example, Augustine could not go back to some established theology of Original Sin . . . there simply was no such theology at that time. It was largely through this discussion with the Pelagians that such a theology had its beginnings. Augustine argued, correctly, that no one could save himself by his own efforts, but that all were in need of the saving intervention of God's grace in our lives. This was in complete contrast to the Pelagian position, which argued that man could take the initial and fundamental steps towards his salvation through his own efforts. In answer to Augustine's more biblical claims, the Pelagians argued from experience. They asked just how an innocent child, newly-born and never having committed sin, needed the grace of Christ. Augustine struggled for a long time with this problem, but his final solution was that essential to the conception of a child, even among Christian married couples, was concupiscence. All children are born within the context of a physical desire, concupiscence, and thus do not belong to God but to the world. As he wrote in 419:

> Because of this concupiscence it comes to pass that even from just and rightful marriages of the children of God, not children of God but children of the world are born (*De nuptiis et concupiscentia* I,18,20).

It is easy enough for us today, looking back over nearly two thousand years of Christian theology, to point out that the identification which Augustine made between concupiscence and sinfulness was where he made his mistake (as did Luther after him), but Augustine did not have nearly two thousand years of Christian tradition to enlighten him. He was founding that tradition! Thus, he must be understood within his own historical context and the extremely positive overall argument which he was pursuing. He was insisting upon the universal need for the grace of Christ. The discussion over infants only arose as a codicil to that argument. He also tended to react strongly against his former days as a Manichean, a sect which gave fleshly matters little importance and which was thus indifferent to either great asceticism or great libertinism. Both extremes are to be found among the Manichees. Nevertheless, despite all these conditioning factors, Augustine still reflects the rather negative stance taken towards marriage by some of the earlier Fathers. Their generally felt view of marriage became very fixed in the Christian tradition, to which Augustine necessarily belonged, although it never became a major part of the early Church's teaching. Very emphatic were the ideas of a man like Tertullian (about 160-225) whose hard line on matters of sexual activity and marriage eventually led him out of the mainstream Christian Church into a sect called Montanism (about 211-212). Given the widespread favour which these opinions had in the early centuries (although very few were as extreme as Tertullian), it is remarkable evidence of the presence of a guiding Spirit in the Church that such positions *never* became the central teaching of the Church on the Sacrament of marriage, even though traces of it have always managed to creep into some lesser legislation, down to our own days.

Nevertheless, even though the Christian Church has retained her balance remarkably well over the centuries, it must be granted that the "traditional" interpretation of Matt. 19,12; I Cor. 7,32-35 and the almost unanimous opinion of the Fathers of the Church have left a powerful impression upon Christian thought and practice. The Council of Trent picked up that tradition and condemned the Reformers' polemical attack upon the Religious state within the Church by claiming that virginity was a superior state of life (*Trent on the Sacrament of Marriage*, Canon 10). Contemporary historical criticism is questioning the value of *all* of the sources for this long-held view which still creates an unhealthy distance between the vowed celibate and the vowed married person, with the latter under the impression that his or her form of life is in some way inferior. As we shall see, it is possible that Matt. 19,12 — at least within the argument which the evangelist Matthew is pursuing at that stage of his Gospel — has nothing to do with the chastity of some who commit themselves to a vowed life of celibacy. St. Paul's teaching in I Cor. 7 appears to have been heavily influenced by his belief that the end time was to come very soon. This belief proved to be incorrect, and Paul was quite prepared to modify his views. As this is the case, the argument of I Cor. 7,32-35 loses its force somewhat. Of course, both Matt. 19,12 and I Cor. 7,32-35 must be read within their wider context. Too often they are simply cited as the final word on the issue, with little or no sensitivity to what the authors themselves were trying to say. This can only be appreciated properly through a reading of the whole of the author's argument. There is also a widespread insistence that we understand the Fathers of the Church within the context of their own times. The early Church unconsciously reflected the decadent late Roman world and it reacted powerfully to the debauchery and general sexual licence which was so much part and parcel of that era. It is also important to understand how their theology of virginity is closely related to — and is a continuation of — the theology of martyrdom. In the first two centuries of the Christian Church's existence, martyrdom loomed large as a pastoral problem. The early writers of the Church necessarily faced this problem and wrote beautifully of its significance for an authentic life of discipleship. However, when the phenomenon of martyrdom lessened, this theology passed unconsciously and easily into the reflections of the Fathers upon a life of virginity. This was to prove a most valuable contribution to the growth of Christian thought, but we must be very careful not to settle for the Fathers' teachings about the superiority of virginity, and simply universalise that teaching for all men and women of all times. That would be to lack all historical and critical sense in our use of our traditions. The same has to be said for the Canon from the Council of Trent. To understand this canon (and any other Church teaching), it must be read as a direct response to a pastoral problem. Once one is aware of the detail and method of the Reformers' attack upon the Religious state, then the canon can be read as a valid defence of that state. However, the canon cannot be properly understood or applied outside the context of that polemic from the 16th century. It appears, therefore, that we must look again at our sources to see if a helpful, guiding teaching on the sense and purpose of a life committed to chaste celibacy can be rediscovered. Although I have touched upon the problems of the early tradition and the Council of Trent, I must now limit myself to a reappraisal of what Vatican II and the Gospels have to offer.

Vatican II

Given the beautiful teaching which came from Vatican II on the holiness of the chaste life of conjugal love, we have every right to look to the contemporary teaching of the Church for guidance as we attempt to develop a theology of a life of vowed chaste celibacy within the Church. The question is dealt with explicitly in the document on the Renewal of the Religous Life:

> Chastity "for the sake of the Kingdom of heaven" (Matt. 19,12) which religious profess, must be esteemed an exceptional gift of grace. It uniquely frees the heart of man (cf. I Cor. 7, 32-35), so that he becomes more fervent in love for God and for all men. For this reason it is a special symbol of heavenly benefits, and for religious it is a most effective means of dedicating themselves wholeheartedly to the divine service and the works of the apostolate (*Perfectae Caritatis*, 12).

The Religious, having read of the wonders of married love, "caught up into divine love", in *Gaudium et Spes*, 48, has every reason for feeling a little disappointed with this rather prosaic treatment of the life of chaste celibacy. The number then goes on with a series of warnings:

> Religious, at pains to be faithful . . .
> they should not presume on their own strength . . .
> they should practise mortification and custody of the senses.
> Nor should they neglect the natural means which promote health of mind and body.
> They should not be influenced by false doctrines.
> Candidates ought not to go forward . . . except after really adequate testing . . . (!)
> warned against the dangers to chastity.

I am not, of course, claiming that *any* of this is wrong, but we may have expected something a little more positive. The general atmosphere of danger, caution and fear does not help us a great deal in our attempt to formulate and live a positive and joyful theology of chaste celibacy. Unfortunately, the same sort of atmosphere pervades another major treatment of this question in the document on the training of Priests (see *Optatam Totius*, 10), although the section on the chastity of the Religious in the document on the Church is sounder and more positive (see *Lumen Gentium*, 42-43). However, *Perfectae Caritatis*, 12 and *Optatam Totius*, 10 are misleading on a far more important issue than their negative tone. Taking up the tradition, the Council has used Matt. 19,12 and I Cor. 7,32-35, interpreting these texts to mean that chaste celibacy "frees the heart of man", and is thus "a most effective means of dedicating themselves wholeheartedly to the divine service and the works of the apostolate". *Optatam Totius* claims that a formation to celibacy will enable the candidates to "acquire greater mastery of mind and body" and to "grow in maturity and receive greater measure of the blessedness promised by the Gospel". Both documents speak very well of a celibate (although they say "chaste") life being an important eschatological sign, and this is very true. Nevertheless, one of the major ideas conveyed is plainly that celibacy is a means by which the Religious or the Priest is freed from the encumbrance of a family so that he or she may be able to work and pray more effectively, and thus earn a greater share in God's love and grace. I believe that this is to misinterpret the biblical evidence used (Matt. 19,12 and I Cor. 7,32-35), but it also poses serious problems at a practical level. If the chaste celibate is able to come closer to God in work and prayer because of his or her celibacy, and thus "receive greater measure of the blessedness promised by the Gospel" (*Optatam Totius*, 10), where does that put the chaste married person? Logic would force us to conclude that their being married, their being non-celibate, must take them further away from God and his gracious gifts. Such a conclusion is, of course, in obvious contradiction to the teaching of the Bible (especially Eph. 5,21-33) and of the Church: "Authentic married love is caught up into divine love and is directed and enriched by the redemptive power of Christ and the salvific action of the Church" (*Gaudium et Spes*, 48). Surely such a position needs some serious rethinking?

It may seem strange to the every-day reader of what I have just written that such contradictions can be found in the official documents of an ecumenical council. A slight knowledge of how such a council works — with the commissions and sub-commissions actually writing the documents with the assembled Bishops reading, discussing and approving them only very late in their development — should help.

The remarkable feature of the extremely complicated organisation of Vatican II is not the contradictions . . . but the lack of them!

Quite apart from all the possible exegetical niceties, and the various theological interpretations which can arise from our extremely rich tradition, there remains a further glaring difficulty which most celibates must feel when faced with such teaching: it is a contradiction of our own experience of life. The chaste and fruitful love of dedicated and loyal married couples has always been one of the most wonderful places for the revelation of the love of God among men and women of all ages. One can only conclude that while chaste married love is beautifully dealt with in *Gaudium et Spes*, much more has to be done on the biblical and theological motivation for chaste celibacy.

Contemporary Biblical Criticism of Matt. 19,12 and I Cor. 7,32-35

I have already mentioned that there is some doubt among biblical scholars as to whether it is correct to use these passages as the biblical background and support for a life of chaste celibacy — especially when they are used to argue that such a form of life is a superior form of Christian life. I wish to approach this biblical material in two steps. First I would like to show how the application of modern biblical methods seriously questions the traditional conclusions drawn from them. Secondly, I will attempt to show that it is possible, after all, to rediscover a more positive and realistic theology and practice of chaste celibacy *from the same texts*.

Matthew 19,12

As in all literary criticism, this famous passage on being a "eunuch" must not be pulled out of its context and explained as if it were the only thing which Matthew reported from Jesus. It has a place in the Gospel as a whole, and also within its own immediate context. It has been precisely the study of Matthew 19,12 within its own literary context which has led contemporary scholars to seriously question whether the passage is correctly used to speak of chaste celibacy. Although the reader may find some of the following suggestions quite novel, it is important to know that I am carrying further here an approach to this passage that was initiated in 1959 by Dom Jacques Dupont, O.S.B.

As we have already seen from our study of the story of the rich man, Matthew has used Mark's Gospel as a source for a great deal of his own Gospel. We have also already seen, from our study of that passage, that Matthew is capable of rewriting Mark's version of the events with a great deal of skill, in order to make the message of the narrative appeal more directly to the situation of his own particular community. A careful reading of Mark 10,1-12 and Matt. 19,1-12 will show that Matt. 19,12 comes as the final statement in a passage which Matthew has largely constructed from his major source: Mark's Gospel.

Matthew 19,1-12	*Mark 10,1-12*
1. Now when Jesus had finished these sayings, he went away from Gaililee and entered the region of Judea beyond the Jordan; 2. and large crowds followed him and he healed them there.	1. And he left there and went to the region of Judea and beyond the Jordan, and crowds gathered to him again; and again, as his custom was, he taught them.
3. And Pharisees came up to him and tested him by asking, "Is it lawful to divorce one's wife for any cause?"	2. And Pharisees came up and in order to test him asked, "Is it lawful for a man to divorce his wife?" 3. He answered them, "What did Moses command you?" 4. They said, "Moses allowed a man to write a certificate of divorce, and to put her away." 5. But Jesus said to them, "For your hardness of heart he wrote you this commandment.
(see below, vv 7-8)	

4. He answered, "Have you not read that he who made them from the beginning made them male and female, 5. and said, 'For this reason a man shall leave his father and mother and be joined to his wife, and the two shall become one'? 6. So they are no longer two but one. What therefore God has joined together, let not man put asunder". 7. They said to him, "Why then did Moses command one to give a certificate of divorce, and to put her away?" 8. He said to them, "For your hardness of heart Moses allowed you to divorce your wives, but from the beginning it was not so.

9. And I say to you: whoever divorces his wife, except for unchastity, and marries another, commits adultery.

10. The disciples said to him, "If such is the case of a man with his wife, it is not expedient to marry". 11. But he said to them, "Not all men can receive this precept, but only those to whom it is given. 12. For there are eunuchs who have been so from birth, and there are eunuchs who have been

6. But from the beginning of creation 'God made them male and female'. 7. 'For this reason a man shall leave his father and mother and be joined to his wife, 8. and the two shall become one'. So they are no longer two but one. 9. What therefore God has joined together, let not man put asunder".

(see above, vv. 3-5)

10. And in the house the disciples asked him again about this matter. 11. And he said to them, "Whoever divorces his wife and marries another, commits adultery against her; 12. and if she divorces her husband and marries another, she commits adultery".

made eunuchs by men, and there are eunuchs who have made themselves eunuchs for the sake of the kingdom of heaven. He who is able to receive this, let him receive it".

After differing geographical indications (although Matt. 19,1 is probably an attempt to clarify the confused geography of Mark 10,1) and rather stereotyped Marcan and Matthean expressions in v. 2 of both versions, the reader will notice that the first nine verses of Matthew's account follow Mark 10,3-12. They both report a discussion between Jesus and the Pharisees over divorce. Although Matthew has not followed Mark's order in the discussion (Mark 10,3-5 has been transferred to Matt. 19,7-8, as this suits Matthew's presentation of the narrative in the form of a rabbinic discussion), and he has not followed Mark word for word, practically everything (with an important exception in v. 9) in Matt. 19,3-9 comes from his source, Mark 10,3-12. However, a glance at the two passages, as I have arranged them in parallel, shows that Matthew's final three verses (vv. 10-12) have *no parallel* in Mark. In fact, they are not reported anywhere else in the whole of the New Testament. This should already put us on our guard. Although Matthew was quite happy to tell his community of the encounter which Jesus had with the Pharisees over the question of divorce (vv. 3-9), and he went to his usual source, Mark, for that account, he found that there was still more to be said on the matter. As Mark's account (Mark 10,1-12) did not deal with *all* the issues which Matthew felt needed explanation, he added vv. 10-12. In short, if Matt. 19,10-12 is a passage which the evangelist added to his source, Mark 10,1-12, as is obvious from a study of the two texts in parallel, then Matthew wished to say something which Mark had left unsaid.

Let us now examine Matt. 19,3-12, keeping an eye particularly on his rewriting of the Gospel of Mark. In Matthew's account particular attention has been given to a presentation of the encounter between Jesus and the Pharisees as a form of a rabbinic discussion. In the first century there was a discussion among the various rabbinic schools over the causes for divorce. There were basically two lines of thought. A Rabbi Shammai argued (through an interpretation of Deut. 24,1) that one could only divorce one's wife when there was a serious moral reason for such an action. On the other hand, a Rabbi Hillel (through a sophisticated interpretation of the same passage, Deut. 24,1) claimed that a divorce was possible for any reason at all. The Mishnah, a Jewish document which presents this discussion, informs us that, for Hillel, it was sufficient reason if the wife spoiled the cooking, or if there was a more attractive person available (see, *Gittin* 9,10). Once we have this background clear, then the question of Matthew 19,3 makes a great deal of sense: "Is it lawful to divorce one's wife *for any cause*?" Jesus' opinion is being sought in a current discussion over the important question of divorce. However, both Matthew and Mark make it clear that the Pharisees, great experts in the Law, are trying to catch him out by placing him in what we nowadays call "a Catch-22 situation". We are told that they "tested him" (Greek: *peirazō*). They obviously ask whether or not he agrees with Rabbi Hillel's argument. If he does, then they will declare that he is wrong, and take up the position of Shammai, but if he does not, then they will defend Hillel's claims. Jesus is placed, apparently, in a "no-win" position. Jesus' answer follows good rabbinic practice, as he quotes from the Law of Moses (Gen. 1,27 and 2,24), but he then interprets these texts in a way which cuts across the question of the reasons for divorce by saying that divorce is impossible: "What therefore God has joined together, let no man put asunder" (Matt. 19,4-6). Remarkably, Jesus' answer indicates that the whole discussion between Shammai and Hillel is irrelevant — both are wrong!

The Pharisees, not to be beaten, also go to the Law of Moses (Deut. 24,1: the basic text in the Shammai-Hillel debate) and ask why a bill of divorce was allowed by Moses, if there was to be no divorce (v. 7). Jesus replies that it was because of the hardness of the heart of Israel that this happened. He then abandons all reference to the Law of Moses and announces: "And I say to you". Throughout Matthew's Gospel we find Jesus teaching in this way. All discussions of the Law, which Jesus has come to bring to its perfection (see 5,17: "Think not that I have come to abolish the law and the prophets; I have come not to abolish them but to fulfil them") ultimately end with Jesus' new and radical reinterpretation based *entirely* on his word. The Matthean Jesus repeatedly proclaims: "And I say to you" (see, especially, 5,22. 26. 28. 32. 34. 39. 44). Thus, abandoning all reference to the old Law, and entirely upon the authority of his own word, Jesus teaches:

> Whoever divorces his wife, except for unchastity, and marries another, commits adultery (v. 9).

Jesus lays down a prohibition of divorce, allowing only one exception. It is important for us to notice, at this stage, that Mark 10,11, which Matthew is following here, allows of no exception. Mark is absolute: "Whoever divorces his wife and marries another, commits adultery against her". In fact, the rest of the New Testament (see I Cor. 7,10-11; Luke 16,18) is absolute in its prohibition of divorce. Only Matthew, therefore, has added this exception. We now find that Matthew has made two major alterations to his source:

a) He has added "except for unchastity" as he rewrote Mark 10,11 in v. 9.

b) He has also added three verses (vv. 10-12) which lead up to and include the eunuch saying in v. 12. They are not found in Mark.

We must ask why Matthew added these very important passages, but first let us take our analysis further.

We are now in the passage (vv. 10-12) which is found only in Matthew. The disciples are stunned by the severity of Jesus' teaching and they exclaim: "If such is the case of a man with his wife, it is expedient not to marry" (v. 10). Translated into modern terms (and practice!) the disciples are saying: "If I am unable to get rid of a wife, then I will be better off if I do not marry her in the first place!" This is a perfectly logical and common-sense response to Jesus' prohibition of divorce, as long as one is working from purely human criteria, but Jesus' answer to this objection (v. 11) is to point out that it is no longer "the case of a man with his wife". What he has just announced is an entirely new situation which cannot be measured by human, social and sexual criteria. He is talking about the wonderful gift which is called *Christian* marriage: "Not all men can *receive* this precept, but only those to whom it is *given*" (v. 11). We are no longer dealing with the human, social and sexual situation of a man with a woman, but the "graced" situation, the gift of Christian marriage. It is its specifically Christian character which makes it indissoluble. It is extremely difficult to capture, in translation, all that Jesus' words imply. We are forced to translate "not all men can *receive* this precept", but Matthew's choice of words here (using a Greek verb *chōreō*) illustrates beautifully the "givenness", of Christian marriage. It is quite correctly translated as "receive", in an intellectual sense, but it also carries with it the idea of "to make space for" (see also Mark 2,2 and Matt. 15,17 where the verb is used with this "spatial" sense). In this way, the idea of being "open" to a gift which is given is conveyed. We then come to v. 12:

> For there are eunuchs who have been so from birth,
> and there are eunuchs who have been made eunuchs by men,
> and there are eunuchs who have made themselves eunuchs
> for the sake of the Kingdom of heaven.
> He who is able to receive this, let him receive it.

What are we to make of this passage in a context which is *entirely* made up of a discussion of divorce? If the passage is about consecrated celibacy, as has been traditionally believed, how does it relate to the rest of its context? We have just seen that vv. 3-11 are concerned with the question of divorce. In Matt. 19,13 a short section on the relationship between children and the Kingdom of heaven begins. This problem has led scholars to seek a variety of solutions, but we must go back to the fact that Matthew, who is largely following Mark 10,3-12, has made those two important additions: "except for unchastity" in v. 9 and the passage leading up to and including our eunuch passage in vv. 10-12. If Matthew has added these passages, then we must suppose that he has done so for a purpose. There must have been some urgent pastoral concern in the community for which he wrote his Gospel that he was trying to assist by these additions.

It is nowadays generally admitted that the Gospel of Matthew was written for a community largely composed of Jewish-Christians, facing difficulties on two fronts:

a) The expulsion from the ancient Torah-centered life-style when official Judaism gradually came to see that any sect which believed that the expected Messiah had already come in Jesus of Nazareth could not possibly remain within the ranks of Judaism. Gradually, there was a once-and-for-all break between the Christian Church and the Synagogue.

b) The Christian message, based in the life, death and resurrection of a Jew, preached and lived in a largely Jewish context throughout its first generation, was now being preached to the Gentiles. Indeed the Matthean community saw the preaching of the Christian message to "all the nations" as an essential part of their response to Jesus (see, especially, Matt. 28,16-20). This meant, however, that there were many ex-Gentiles coming into the Matthean community without any formation in the basically Jewish thought and tradition which stood at the heart of the early Christian message.

It seems that Matthew had to face two serious problems in questions of Christian marriages among those Gentiles who came into his community without any Jewish background or formation. It is important to notice that *both* of the difficulties which the Matthean community faced have been dealt with in Matt. 19,3-12. The major part of the discussion over divorce, taken from Mark, dealt with Jesus' reinterpretation of Torah, the Law of Moses. This is the subject of the rabbinic discussion between Jesus and the Pharisees. However, the two additions to Mark 10,3-12 are an attempt to handle difficulties that were peculiar to the Matthean community.

In the first place, there were some who were married in a way which Jewish Law (see Lev. 18,6-18) regarded as incestuous. We have a clear indication that this was happening in the early Christian Church from Paul's discussion of it in I Cor. 5,1-5. Exactly the same expression which Matthew uses to speak of "unchastity" in v. 9 (Greek: *porneia*) is used by Paul to speak of the incestuous situation of one of the members of the Corinthian community (I Cor. 5,1). In such a situation Matthew allows divorce. This explains why Matthew has added "except for unchastity (*porneia*)" in v. 9. The situation of "unchastity" in which some of his ex-Pagan converts lived could not be tolerated by his largely Jewish-Christian community. What was he to do? The traditional discussion of these questions in Mark 10,11 gave him no solution, as it had not faced his pastoral problem. Thus he had to fall back upon what was basically a Jewish law: there is to be no divorce, except in those cases which were judged to be incestuous by the traditional Jewish law, even though they may have been perfectly normal in the Pagan culture from which the new Christians had come.

But this was not the only problem which the ex-Pagan converts seemed to be creating for the community. Once we have seen that Matthew's community was struggling to work out a new legislation on marital situations which were arising among their ex-Gentile converts in the addition of "except for unchastity" to a previous absolute prohibition of divorce, then we probably have a good indication of why Matthew added vv. 10-12 to his source. There would have been some ex-Gentiles who had come into the Christian community and married there, understanding marriage in the way described by Jesus in v. 11: the giftedness and uniqueeness of a Christian sacrament. However, such a vision does not always remain. There would have been some who, at a later stage, became disenchanted with this strange new approach to God, and who would have left the confines of the Matthean community, returning to their former situations of culture, religion and marital practice. The problem that Matthew seems to be facing here is that one of the partners of the Christian marriage has remained within the Christian community. According to Matt. 19,3-9 such a person is still linked to his or her former partner through the bond of a Christian marriage. Here it is important to remember that Matthew was writing for a concrete Christian community, probably somewhere in Syria in the 80's of the first century. While one partner was attempting to work out life within the Christian community, his or her ex-partner was in the same village or town, living a form of Pagan life which the Christian partner had decided to abandon. The couple would inevitably meet; their friends would be watching the behaviour of the person who belonged to this strange new sect which followed the way of Jesus of Nazareth. How did Matthew solve this particular problem? He took a very hard line, and asked them to remain unmarried. To those left partnerless in the Matthean community, abandoned by the wife or the husband who had returned to Paganism, Matthew asked that they become "eunuchs for the sake of the Kingdom of heaven" (19,12), i.e., that they do not remarry, but that, despite the pain, they remain loyal to the ideals of Christian marriage indicated by the words of Jesus in v. 11. Matthew was well aware that what he was asking was extremely difficult, in fact impossible, were it not for the grace of God. Therefore, he catches up v. 11 once again, adding: "He who is able to receive this, let him receive it", and then, a little later in the same context, the words of encouragement:

> With men this is impossible,
> but with God all things are possible (19,26).

It appears to me that this is the best explanation of Matt. 19,12 because it solves the problems which Matt. 19,3-12 has always presented to interpreters:

a) To explain why Matthew inserted his exception clause to 19,9 and his addition in vv. 10-12.

b) What is more important is that it explains *both* additions to his Marcan source by relating them to the *same* pastoral problem: the difficulties faced by the irregular marital situations created by the presence in a largely Jewish community of a growing group of ex-Pagan converts.

c) It explains v. 12 within the context of vv. 3-12. It is not to be regarded as a strange, contextless saying, coming at the end of a passage dealing with divorce. The whole passage, from v. 3 right through to v. 12 deals with the theology and practice of marriage and divorce within the Matthean community.

The problem with this explanation, however, is that the traditional use of Matt. 19,12 can no longer be made. We must note carefully what we have seen so far. Up to this point, I have examined what *Matthew* was saying in Matt. 19,3-12. My concern has been to rediscover the *situation within the Matthean Church* which would have caused the evangelist to rewrite Mark in such a striking fashion, and then to understand just what it was that *Matthew* was asking from *his community* in such a situation. The most important guide in such a study has been Matthew's use of Mark 10,3-12. I pointed out that vv. 3-9 came from Mark 10,3-12 . . . but where did Matthew find v. 12, the famous eunuch saying? Did he invent it? There are very good reasons which indicate that he did not, but we will return to that after a consideration of 1 Cor. 7,32-35.

I Cor. 7,32-35

The second passage widely used in the traditional discussion of the celibate state, I Cor. 7,32-35, seems to show clearly that Paul advocated the state of chaste celibacy as a superior state for Christians:

> I want you to be free from anxieties. The unmarried man is anxious about the affairs of the Lord, how to please the Lord; but the married man is anxious about worldly affairs, how to please his wife, and his interests are divided. And the unmarried woman or girl is anxious about the affairs of the Lord, how to be holy in body and spirit; but the married woman is anxious about worldly affairs, how to please her husband. I say this for your own benefit, not to lay any restraint upon you, but to promote good order and to secure your undivided devotion to the Lord.

Once again, however, we must be extremely careful not to read this very important text as if it were the only thing which Paul had ever written. It has a context within I Cor. 7, within the overall argument of the letter itself, and then within the overall context of the development of Paul's own thought. The passage which immediately precedes 7,32-35 should already show that there is much more to the question, as Paul writes of a whole series of worldly and human activities which must become relative:

> I think that *in view of the impending distress* it is well for a person to remain as he is . . . I mean, brethren, that *the appointed time has grown very short*; from now on let those who have wives live as though they had none, and those who mourn live as though they were not mourning, and those who rejoice as though they were not rejoicing, and those who buy as though they had no goods, and those who deal with the world as though they had no dealings with it. *For the form of this world is passing away* (I Cor. 7,26.29-31).

In this passage Paul gives his reasons why he believes that the Corinthians should drop all attention and concern over a series of every-day affairs: wives, mourning, rejoicing, possessions and commerce. The reasons for such a relativising of every day concerns are also given:

— in view of the impending distress
— the appointed time has grown very short
— the form of this world is passing away.

What does Paul mean by such expressions? It appears that he was writing under the urgent conviction that some sort of great cataclyism was about to strike the world. In fact, it is clear that the early Paul was convinced and urged on in his preaching of certain matters because he believed that the final end of all time, to be understood as the return of the Lord in the Christian view of things, was only just around the corner. It is evident from his first letters, the letters to the Thessalonians, possibly written in the early 50's, that he had preached his message of the imminent return of the Lord with such conviction that the Christians in Thessalonia had decided that all they had to do was sit and wait! There was no need for them to apply themselves to their day to day tasks, if the Day of the Lord was about to fall upon them. This is the sort of situation which led Paul to write so clearly: "if any one will not work, let him not eat" (II Thess. 3,10). The first letter to the Thessalonians faced the even more serious question of the fate of those Christians who had already died, before the return of the Lord (see, especially, I Thess. 4,13-5,11).

The first letter to the Corinthians was probably written shortly after the correspondence with Thessalonia, still in the first half of the 50's. Throughout I Corinthians, and especially here, we find that Paul is still caught up by the urgency of the times . . . "the appointed time has grown very short" (v.29). It is because of this conviction that he can so strongly advocate, as a personal opinion, which he carefully distinguishes from a "command" of the Lord, that his Corinthian community devote all their attention — not to wives, husbands, mourning, rejoicing, buying, selling and dealing with the world (see vv. 26-31) - but to the Lord, who is about to come (vv. 32-35). But he did not come . . . and he still has not come, in the sense intended by Paul and understood by his audience. If Paul's teaching on the advantages (superiority?) of the celibate state is so intimately linked with his presupposition that the end of the time is near at hand, does this teaching not become somewhat relative when such a presupposition proves to be false? In fact, Paul's own understanding of the end of time develops. He was able to see, as the years passed by, that the Church was about to face a long history, and thus several of his positions in his later letters (especially the so-called "Prison Letters": Ephesians, Philippians, Colossians) vary from those found in the Thessalonian and Corinthian correspondence. If the end time is near at hand, there is no urgent need for a theology of marriage. However, if the Church is going to work its way successfully through a long history, then such a theology is urgently needed. While I Cor. 7 reflects the teaching of the early Paul, the letter to the Ephesians represents a superb systematic reflection on the essence of his message, even though it may have been finally written after Paul had already died. Thus, in Eph. 5,21-33 we find:

> Be subject to one another out of reverence for Christ. Wives, be subject to your husbands as to the Lord. For the husband is the head of the wife as Christ is the head of the Church, his body, and is himself its saviour. As the Church is subject to Christ, so let wives also be subject in everything to their husbands. Husbands, love your wives as Christ loved the Church and gave himself up for her, that he might sanctify her, having cleansed her by the washing of water with the word, that he might present the Church to himself in splendour, without spot or wrinkle or any such thing, that she might be holy and without blemish. Even so husbands should love their wives as their own bodies. He who loves his wife loves himself . . . This mystery is a profound one, and I am saying that it refers to Christ and the Church; however, let each one of you love his wife as himself, and let the wife see that she respects the husband.

As the reader will be quick to recognise, such powerfully *positive* teaching has provided the Church with the sort of theology of the married state which stands behind *Gaudium et Spes*, 48.

Having said all this, however, a word of warning must be issued. We must not rule out of court the central point of Paul's teaching in this treatment. Notice that he states his purpose in v. 32: "I want you to be free from anxieties". Anything which stands between the Christian and his total adhesion to the Lord must be regarded as secondary. Paul is not praising the celibate state because of some intrinsic virtue inherent in that physical situation. To interpret the passage in this way is to miss the point. Paul links the celibate vocation with wholehearted devotion and prayerful attention to the Lord. The beautiful phrase concluding v. 35: "to secure your undivided devotion to the Lord" evokes that attitude of Mary in the Martha and Mary story (see Luke 10,38-42). The image, both in Paul and Luke, is that of the Christian absorbed in attention at the feet of the Lord. Paul is not *primarily* concerned with the relative merits of the married or the celibate state; he is concerned that his Christians be one in joy, love and hope, freed from any anxieties (see v. 32) which may destroy the all-important factor, their "life in Christ". The marriage discussion has arisen as a *Corinthian* problem (one of many!), and again we must be careful not to absolutise the wrong issue. The only thing that matters for Paul is that his Christians be consumed by an "undivided devotion to the Lord" (v. 35). As we shall see shortly, here Paul is close to Jesus' own understanding of the function of a celibate life within the universal Gospel imperative of Christian chastity.

Nevertheless, we still find that a study of the whole context of the passage used traditionally in discussions of the celibate state within the Christian Church rather lessens its significance. Are we, then, without any biblical support for this state of life in the Church? Is it possible that such an important feature of Christian tradition and practice has come about because of some strange mentality in the early Church, where the times and the world in which it was growing led it into an undervaluation of God's creation and the place of human love, affection and fruitfulness. This is difficult to accept, and the most serious contra-indication is the permanence of the charism of chaste celibacy in the

Church throughout the whole of its history. Such phenomena do not usually have their origins in a mistaken view. At this stage of our considerations we must return to a further analysis of Matt. 19,12.

The Eunuch Saying on the Lips of Jesus

As I concluded my treatment of what the eunuch passage meant within the context of Matt. 19,3-12, I asked the question: Where did Matthew find v. 12? Did he invent it, or did it come to him from some source? It is widely accepted that Matthew did *not* invent 19,12, but that he found it among the remembered words of Jesus of Nazareth himself. Scholars have various criteria for determining whether or not certain passages were composed in the early Church, or whether they came from Jesus himself. The following are the main reasons which have led most scholars to conclude that — no matter what use the evangelist has made of it within Matt. 19,3-12 — it was something which was originally said by Jesus of Nazareth during his public ministry:

a) The word "eunuch" is an extremely harsh expression. It is a difficult enough word today, but in the first century, when such men were a public part of society — even though a rejected part of that society — it was extremely offensive and crude. There is not the slighest possibility that the early Church would have ever invented a saying which used such an expression, to place it upon the lips of Jesus, as he spoke of himself or his followers. You do not have your heroes described (or describing themselves) with offensive language. If the saying is found in the Gospel of Matthew, then it must have been said by Jesus. Despite the continual repetition of the word "eunuch" in Matt. 19,12, the evangelist has been able to take it from the tradition and use it — because Jesus himself had said it.

b) The structure of the passage is typical of a semitic proverb, where the listener (or reader) is gradually led through a rhythmic play on a word, not knowing exactly where it is going to end. The point of the proverb is then made in the final phrase. This proverbial form is called a *mashal*, and even in an English translation one can sense how Jesus used this literary form:

> There are *eunuchs* . . .
> and there are *eunuchs*
> who have been made *eunuchs* . . .
> and there are *eunuchs*
> who have made themselves *eunuchs*
> *for the sake of the kingdom of heaven.*

This "form" of the saying takes us back to an Aramaic-speaking background.

c) Although Luke and Mark (understandably) do not report this passage, it has returned in Christian tradition, *in a slightly different form*, in the writings of Justin Martyr (about 100-165) and St. Epiphanius (about 315-403), two early Fathers of the Church. This suggests that they had also heard or seen this passage, but as they reproduce it in a different form from Matt. 19,12, they probably had it from an independent source. This also indicates that Matthew did not invent it; it existed independently of Matt. 19,12.

As the reader will have sensed, the most important element in our rediscovery of the origins of this saying is to be found in the impossibility of a situation in the life of the early Church where such a saying would have been invented and placed upon the lips of Jesus. It must be there because Jesus said it. However, if he said it, then we must try to step back yet further, and ask why he said it, what was the situation in his life which created such a saying and — most important of all — what did such a saying mean to him.

The attitude of people in first century Judaism towards eunuchs was extremely negative. Deut. 23,1 forbids the presence of a eunuch among God's chosen people, and both Jewish and pagan literature present them as sycophantish, fat, beardless, feminine — but despotically cruel. Nevertheless, the "eunuch" theme is central to Matt. 19,12. Despite its crudeness and its offensive implications, it is used, either as a verb or a noun, no less than five times in this one verse. Why would Jesus use such an expression?

There is ample evidence in the Gospels that Jesus was the object of continual abuse from his opponents. He and his disciples did not fast (Mark 2,18), they violated the Sabbath (Mark 2,23) and they took their meals without the ritual lustrations (Mark 7,5). Jesus himself is called "a glutton and a drunkard, a friend of tax collectors and sinners" (Matt. 11,19). "You are a Samaritan and have a demon", accuse the Jews in John 8,48, and on another occasion we are told that "they have called the master of the household Beelzebul" (Matt. 10,25). It appears that this process of heaping abuse upon Jesus was a very common approach among his opponents (for further indications, see M. Hengel, *The Charismatic Leader and His Followers* [Edinburgh, T. & T. Clark, 1981] pp. 38-42). Among the many terms used for such abuse it appears more than likely that they would have called Jesus "eunuch!". Given the importance of marriage and the procreation of children, in obedience to Gen. 1,28, there must have been something unique about the life of Jesus of Nazareth which gave his opponents the opportunity to call him a eunuch, in a derogatory and abusive sense. There is only one known celibate Rabbi, a certain Ben Azzai, and he was always sharply criticised by other Rabbis for such a way of life. Indeed they also cast suspicion upon his private life, suggesting illicit liaisons with the daughter of one of the great Rabbis, and also that he had been divorced (see, Babylonian Talmud, *Sotah* 4b and *Ketubboth* 63a). It appears to me that Matt. 19,12 on the lips of Jesus was his calm reply to the attacks of his enemies who sought any excuse to hurl abuse at this troublesome character. Jesus was a celibate, but he was also a figure who troubled the establishment by the quality of his life, by his preaching and by his remarkable authority as a miracle worker. Gradually he was attracting a following which looked no longer to the Jewish hierarchy for their leadership. Some sort of attack had to be mounted against him, and —in their view — his celibacy was one of his weak points. They saw in his celibate state a golden opportunity to question the quality of his life, and thus undermine his authority. To do this they called him "eunuch!". I would further suggest that one of the reasons why this particular "word of Jesus" remained alive in the pre-Matthean tradition, despite the harshness of the word "eunuch", was because it was Jesus' regular answer to a regular form of abuse which was aimed at him. Readers will be well aware that this form of abuse has not died out over the centuries. When all forms of logical and rational argument can no longer win the day, all languages and cultures with which I am familiar turn readily to a form of abuse which attacks a man's sexual capacities. My own Australian "popular culture" is extremely rich in such expressions!

It is not enough to establish, through our modern critical methods, the fact that a celibate Jesus replied to his enemies in the terms of Matt. 19,12. What is most important for us, at this stage of our study, is to task just what the saying meant for Jesus. Earlier we saw that *Matthew* used the saying, within the overall context of his Gospel and 19,3-12, to speak to ex-pagan Christians who had been abandoned by their partners and now found themselves alone — yet, according to the teaching of Jesus in Matt 19,11, could not remarry. However, we have now seen that the passage had its origin on the lips of Jesus, and there it meant something quite different: it was an explanation of why Jesus of Nazareth lived his chastity in a celibate way. We are now touching the heart of our question: a biblical background for the Christian practice of chaste celibacy.

It has been traditional to argue that reason for being a eunuch was "for the sake of the kingdom of heaven" in what could be called a final sense. By this I mean that one chose celibacy so that one might be free, and thus able to give oneself totally to the construction of the kingdom of heaven which was still coming. It was yet to be established, and the decision for celibacy was taken to aid in that task. This is the way *Perfectae Caritatis*, 12 uses Matt. 19,12 and this is the source of my major difficulty with that passage from the Council. The original Greek of the passage in Matthew means much more than that. The Greek uses a certain construction (a preposition *dia* followed by an accusative case) which indicates that Jesus announced to his opponents that he was a eunuch "because of" the kingdom of heaven. He was not a celibate *so that* he might construct the Kingdom to come, but *because of* the Kingdom which was already present in his life (see H. G. Liddell — R. Scott, *A Greek English Lexicon*, p.389: "to express the cause, occasion or purpose"). It is the overwhelming power of the presence of the Kingdom in his life that led Jesus to celibacy. This becomes clearer when we look at the whole of 19,12. Jesus' opponents knew of two types of eunuchs: the one born so and the one made so by man. These people, because of a *prior* disability, were unable to go into a normal married situation. Jesus was also "unable" to enter into a married situation. However, the motive for Jesus' "inability" differs from that of the other two cases. The cause of his inability was not physical. He was so taken over by the urgent presence of the Kingdom that he could do no other than give himself entirely to it. The celibacy of Jesus was not something which he made happen to himself by first deliberating whether or not it should happen, and then deciding in favour of it, so that he would be free to dedicate himself entirely to the construction of the Kingdom *to come*. The causality ran in the opposite direction. In Jesus of Nazareth the guiding principle and the overwhelming experience of his life was the presence of the lordship of God, whom he called "Abba" — Father (see Matt. 11,27; Mark 13,32; 14,36; Luke 11,2 and the whole of the Fourth Gospel). It was this "lordship" which led him to his state of chaste celibacy, to his being a "eunuch *because of*" the overwhelming presence of the Kingdom in his life.

Interestingly, this interpretation can lead us back to I Cor. 7,32-35. We saw in our consideration of that passage that Paul argued that marriage (and many other ordinary occupations) had become relative in the light of the imminent return of the Lord. We also saw, however, that contemporary exegesis tends to take the sting out of Paul's claims for the superiority and advisability of the celibate state by pointing out that he was not correct in his ideas about the immediate return of the Lord. By glancing at Eph. 5,21-33 we also saw that Paul was great enough to adapt his theology to the changing needs of the early Church as the years passed and it became obvious that the end time may well be a long time coming. However, a celibacy lived under the urgent presence of the Kingdom of God can again make sense of Paul's argument. As we saw in our analysis of I Cor. 7,32-35, what ultimately concerned Paul was the establishment of a community where all that mattered was "life in Christ", the joy, hope, love and unity which can only be created by an "undivided devotion to the Lord". While contemporary exegesis is correct in claiming that we must not make this an all-determining and all-important New Testament teaching on the relative value of marriage, Paul, like Jesus, shows himself to be living under the divine urgency of the overwhelming presence of the Kingdom. Paul may have been mistaken about the immediate return of the Lord, but he is surely correct when he insists that all that matters is our "life in Christ". As this is the case, there is no need to wait for the end time; the eschatological moment is *now*, because the Lord has taken me over *now*, and such an approach to a chaste celibacy can be an outstanding contribution to a Christian presence in the world. In fact, applying the words of Paul to the experience of Jesus, which we have rediscovered through our study of Matt. 19,12, we can say that Jesus lived his chaste celibacy because of an undivided attention to his Lord, the God of Israel, whom he called his Father (see I Cor. 7,35).

The Function of the Vow of Chaste Celibacy

Thus far I have been discussing how Jesus saw and spoke about *his* celibacy. However, his reply to his opponents is framed in the plural: "there are *eunuchs*". As such it was not just a defence of himself and an explanation of why he was not married. It would have been then, and still remains today, an invitation to all those who hear this quiet reply to strident abuse to consider just what the Kingdom might hold if it has taken over Jesus of Nazareth in such a radical way: he can do no other than remain unmarried because of its crowding into his life. Here is the authentically and radically evangelical basis for a life of chaste celibacy. By means of our long and careful analysis of Matt. 19,3-12 we are now in a position to argue that a life of celibate chastity has its biblical support in the lifestyle of Jesus of Nazareth himself. It does not have to be bolstered up by a shaky interpretation of Matt. 19,12 which makes no sense of its context.

Like Jesus, we too can commit ourselves to chaste celibacy because of the overwhelming presence of God's Kingdom which keeps crowding in on us. In other words, our ongoing decision for chaste celibacy is intelligible as a decision which comes about within the context of a major religious experience. The term "religious experience" is a technical term, and must not be misunderstood. It does not refer to experiences which "religious" people have, or experiences which are limited to Churches! Religious experiences are all those experiences which are somehow out of our control. They are greater than us: love, tears, hope, anguish, joy and laughter. No matter what our religious beliefs — or even our total lack of them — "religious experiences" are part and parcel of the life (and death) of every man and woman. Turning now to one particular form of such an experience, one can ask: why does this particular man marry that particular woman? So many other combinations could have been possible, but something unique has happened between these two people. In an authentic situation, they "fall in love". The English expression is very good, as it is a genuine *falling*, out of human control and measurement. They can do no other. There is a kingdom established between the two of them that renders them existentially incapable of doing anything else. All of this happens *before* any decision to marry. Marriage is simply the logical and necessary conclusion to the prior experience of the "falling". So must it be with the decision for chaste celibacy. A life of chaste celibacy is nothing else but the existential consequence which flows out of the prior experience of the urgent presence of the Kingdom of God. This is what it means to be "a eunuch because of the kingdom of heaven" (Matt. 19,12), drawn into a situation where all that matters is that we be "anxious about the affairs of the Lord" (see I Cor. 7,32-35).

A very important consequence of this re-reading of our traditional texts is that it gives the celibate, attempting to live his or her chastity, every right to his or her place in society alongside all classes of men and women, married and unmarried. The celibate must not be regarded as deprived, deformed or in some way "strange". The life of chaste celibacy must never be regarded — by the celibate or by others — as a "stiff-upper-lip" and a "gritting your teeth" business. Where we stand as celibates flows out of exactly the same sort of experience which led that man to marry that woman: the overpowering presence of a kingdom of love. Just as, in an authentic situation of sexual love, the couple can do no other than marry and consecrate themselves to each other and their families through a life of consecrated chastity, so also the celibate, in an authentic situation of celibate love, can do no other than be a "eunuch because of" the kingdom of love in his or her life, in a different but parallel form of consecrated chastity. Seen in this *parallel* fashion, instead of the all-too-familiar *contrasting* fashion, these two different ways of living out the same overpowering experience of loving and being loved can be mutually enriched. The celibate learns from married couples that God's love is revealed through the affective and fruitful love of his creatures, while the married can learn from the life of the celibate that the source of their love ultimately transcends anything that their limited — and often ambiguous —human affection can ever hope to demonstrate.

All Christians are called to a chaste loving. This is the only sort of love which creates. The exhilarating and joyful *total* gift of self and reception of the other, at every level, in an authentic situation of Christian marriage, can only take place within the context of a profound loyalty and trust. As we have seen, the Scriptures parallel it with the gift of Christ for the Church, and the Church says of it that it is "caught up into divine love and is directed and enriched by the redemptive power of Christ and the salvific action of the Church" (*Gaudium et Spes*, 48). Why is this so? What is so special about this "gift" of authentic married love? It gains its uniqueness because of its central function within the sacramental dimensions of the Christian life. Only in marriage do we find the institutionalisation, the public commitment and living out, of one of the major elements in our being made in the image of God (see Gen. 1,26). It is the unique place among men and women where the affective and fruitful nature of a God who is love is revealed to the world. The Gospels tell us that God loved so much that the Incarnation had to burst forth from the immensity of that love (see John 3,16). Love is not love unless it is felt and demonstrated, and this is the commitment of Christian marriage, the vocation to chastity of the major part of Christianity.

Need I list the signs of the times? Sex is used to sell all sorts of innocent wares, and to add spice to an already drugged society. The young are educated to a life-style where to give and to receive in sexual intimacy is like sharing a cup of coffee — as long as both parties think that it may be a useful and enjoyable mutual experience. Marriages and families are collapsing, and the crises among consecrated celibates continues. It is pointless to go on, as we all live —and often wonder at ourselves — in the context of this new dogma of: "If you like it . . . do it!"

Religious, vowed to their particular form of chastity, are not superior in this department. The pain which a celibate life can often cause tells us that. However, we are calling out to a topsy-turvy world that they may have abundant pleasure, but they have lost love. Swept off our feet by the lordship of a God who is love, we show the world that genuine affection is not found in a predatory man or woman hunt, but in the loss of self, as we are taken over by the presence of so great a love that we can do no other than give ourselves uniquely to that love. As I have already said, this does not make it any easier, but from here we can pledge ourselves to a form of a life of love which can speak to all Christians. We can announce, through the joy of a free and unconditional love, that the exquisite experience of loving and belonging to the loved one is not something which we can determine, but is a reflection of the loving gift of a caring, creating, fruitful and loving God. A joyful, loving and enthusiastic consecration to the celibate form of chastity is a living proclamation of one of the basic elements of the Christian faith: "But God shows his love for us in that while we were yet sinners, Christ died for us" (Rom. 5,8). The function of our celibate form of chaste loving is not to produce something different or "odd" within the context of the universal call to the perfection of love (see *Lumen Gentium*, 40). It exists as one of God's gifts to the Church, so that the chaste celibate might call all Christians back to the authentic, faithful, loving and joyful gift of self which is the mark of all Christians . . . celibate or married.

Conclusion

Behind this reinterpretation of our traditional biblical background for a life of chaste celibacy stands the conviction that our celibate form of life gains its source and strength, and only makes sense, from where one stands in one's relationship to God and his overwhelming presence in one's life. Only in this way will such a form of life be a living sign of the presence of the kingdom of a God of love. When this is truly the case, then we will not be afraid to take the risk of loving. Chaste celibate love all too often leads to a spineless "being nice" to everyone, causing the celibate to shy clear of the cut and thrust of the challenge of a genuine closeness to other people. This was not the way of Jesus of Nazareth, and it must not be the way of the people who profess to be his followers. Within the context of our Religious life, our being taken over by the kingdom of love must be seen in the *quality of our life together*. We saw, in our study of evangelical poverty, that our preparedness to share all that we have and all that we are was the measure of an authentic response to the demands of the Gospel. In many ways, the public living out of our chaste celibacy can be reduced to the same thing. We are not *primarily* chaste so that we will be free from the problems of wives and husbands and the difficulties of bringing up children, in order to apply ourselves to some form of apostolic work. As I have already mentioned, *Perfectae Caritatis*, 12 seemed to indicate that this was one of the major functions of chaste celibacy within the Religious life, but I find that very hard to accept. Effective pastoral action will be the *result* of a life lived in a situation of genuine loving. We must be careful not to lose our sense of priorities in this. Jerome Murphy-O'Connor has stated the case well when he wrote:

> It is an unfortunate paradox, but the idea that celibacy frees for universal love is one of the major reasons why religious communities have failed to fulfill their witness potential, because inevitably this gives rise to the view that the community is merely the base *from which* the real work is done. The result is that religious communities become loveless deserts. Not only does this make celibacy virtually impossible because man cannot live without love, but it means that the outsider who is shocked into asking, "What makes them different?", finds nothing but a verbal answer to his question. The real answer, the existential answer, is lacking. Not unnaturally, then, celibate life is judged to be meaningless (*What is Religious Life*? p. 59).

Again, when we come to examine our consciences about the significance of our chaste lives, we must start "at home".

A difficulty in living the life of chaste celibacy is often at the basis of both community and individual crises, and here I would like to return briefly to some of the issues which I raised at the beginning of this chapter. All sorts of lack of love and sinfulness — back-biting conversations, deep divisions among confreres, carelessness about prayer, a lazy living off the hard work of the rest of the community — all this, and many other difficulties in community, are tolerated. A difficulty in the affective area, however, all too often leads to a rapid decision, from the person him or herself and from the community at large, that such a person is "out of place". It is often difficult to find, in these situations, the same tolerance, love and understanding that are given to other problems. In fact, often it is not even a case of tolerance, love and understanding. Often all that is really needed is some plain common sense and straight talking! As far as the New Testament is concerned, discussions of moral issues centre their attention on the basic law of Christianity: the law of love. Among Religious, however, failures against the community, poverty and obedience are tolerated, but we must be careful lest the stern defence of that aspect of our lives which should show the quality of our love should only serve to demonstrate the absence of real love. It is important to remember that in the Gospels, as far as affective problems are concerned, the sinners in question receive no condemnation, but pardon (see especially, Luke 7,36-50 and John 8,1-11). Of course, it may not always be the community which is at fault. Very often, in these difficult situations, many would like to reach out a loving, forgiving and caring hand and heart to the person in difficulty, but the offer is refused. Behind a great deal of this tendency stands the restriction of this vow to the physical state of being a celibate. When physical difficulties arise, people panic, thinking that all is lost and that they have gone beyond the point of no return. This will certainly be the frame of mind where a Religious sees his or her commitment only in terms of "celibacy". However, such need not be the case. We must never be allowed to forget that no matter how sinful we may be, a God of love forgives and calls us back to our commitment to "chastity". The experience of many of us over the difficulties of the recent past must surely indicate the importance of my insistence. Far too many of our friends, fine Religious and Priests, have abandoned their commitment to chastity because of a difficulty in the area of celibacy. We know — and they know — that this was a rash and regrettable decision. I would like to repeat, at this stage of my argument, what I wrote earlier in this chapter: We all have difficulties with poverty and obedience. Most of us are prepared to admit such weaknesses, but we struggle all our lives with them. They seldom lead us into despair. So must it also be with the vow of chastity.

In the light of this, we must learn to be patient with these difficulties, both our own and those of others. It is precisely here that the love and support of the people with whom we live are absolutely vital. Rollo May, the celebrated psychologist, has spoken of the sure sign of a mature and integrated personality as being "the courage of imperfection". We must allow ourselves the exhilaration, genuinely felt and shown, and not just spoken about, which comes from loving and being loved. Only in this way, and through this *experience* can we come closer to an understanding of a God who is defined as "love" (see I John 4,8 and 16). Only then will we be able to see why we can and must be so swept off our feet by the urgent presence of the lordship of such a God.

The celibate must not be seen, either by himself or by others, as outside the experience of genuine human affection. The question of close friendships among celibates arises. There is a growing recognition of this phenomenon within the Religious life and some pastoral and theological research and reflection are now being devoted to it. It is timely, and a knowledge of the history of the Religious life indicates that it is not a new phenomenon (for a good survey, see P. M. Connor, *Celibate Love*, pp. 49-96). It appears to me that there are some basic principles which should govern such relationships.

a) They must not be condemned out of hand. The fear of "particular friendships" should be a thing of the past, although difficulties, mistakes and sinfulness can occur here, as in all aspects of our lives.

b) These friendships must never be sought out. They must arise and happen in a context of mutually shared prayer, work and ideals. A Religious *looking for* a friend will soon find one, usually with painful consequences.

c) Directly related to the point just made, Religious should be extremely careful in establishing close affective bonds with people not committed to celibate chastity. These relationships will almost always begin full of hope and good will, but the person not committed to celibacy understandably has every right to eventually (however subtly) make demands which the celibate cannot hope to fulfill. The person committed to celibate chastity has no right to impose that particular form of chastity upon any one. It can become a serious form of emotional violence.

d) The people in the relationship should be directed by people *outside* the relationship. Again, experience teaches us that self-direction leads to self-deception. This principle is closely related to the need for friends to recognise danger and sinfulness in their relationship. An open and frank sharing with a person outside the relationship is probably the best way for this to be achieved.

These principles may sound simple enough, but they are very difficult to live out in full. It is only possible among people who have their priorities right. Their primary commitment must be to the "life in Christ" which they have in and through their immediate community, their particular Religious family, and the apostolic task which the Church has entrusted to them. Equally important must be their finding and sharing with the God who inspires them to love, in a deep, long and patient, prayer life. Even when all this is part of their lives, the cross will loom large, if their friendship is genuine, because there must always be a readiness to "let go". In this situation, the words of the Psalmist always come to my mind:

> Because he cleaves to me in love,
> I will free him (Ps. 91,14. A.T.).

This may read like poetry, but its reality is extremely painful. It is especially here (but not only here) that one can see the value of the early Church's association of martyrdom theology with virginity. Many Religious are unable to cope with this pain, and relationships run into difficulty, as one or other of the parties tries to possess rather than free the other. As married people would be quick to tell us, it is here that we show our affective immaturity. The married also must be able to "let go". It is one of the most important aspects of a successful and mature conjugal relationship. This is always painful, but it is a pain which frees for authentic, self-giving love. As Kahlil Gibran's *Prophet* said so well:

> Give your hearts, but not into each other's
> keeping.
> For only the hand of Life can contain your
> hearts.
> And stand together yet not too near together:
> For the pillars of the temple stand apart,
> And the oak tree and the cypress grow not in
> each other's shadow.

Although writing of a different matter, William H. Vanstone has written a passage which applies beautifully to this aspect of genuine celibate love:

> Among the circumstances which restrict the expression of love is the capacity of the other to receive. A parent knows the danger of overwhelming or imprisoning a child by expressions of love which are untimely or excessive. A friend knows that expressions of friendship too sudden or demonstrative may simply embarrass. A wife knows that, out of love for her husband, she must sometimes "think about herself". The external restraint which love practises is often a mark of its freedom from internal limit. Love does not lay down the condition that it must be allowed freedom to express itself, nor limit its activity to those circumstances in which it may freely act. Love accepts without limit the discipline of circumstances. Although it always aspires to enlarge its own activity, it sometimes finds its most generous enlargement in the acceptance of restraint. Love must sometimes express itself in the renunciation of not disclosing itself (*Love's*

> *Endeavour, Love's Expense. The Response of Being to the Love of God*, p. 44).

In recent years many close celibate friends have wondered about the ultimate significance of the experience of human love which has come into their celibate lives. Vanstone gives us the answer: "The external restraint which love practises is often a mark of its freedom from internal limit". It must be so, because a chaste celibacy caused by the overpowering experience of the kingdom of a God of love can know no internal limit. I do hope that I have made myself clear. Close affective relationships can be a part of celibate chastity, but they call for an asceticism of the highest order, and must *never* be taken lightly.

Sexual beings, situated in creation and caught up inextricably in God's unfolding history as it works itself out in the lives and in the love of men and women, we are all very conscious that we were made for intimacy. We must face this squarely, convinced that to live properly Christian lives means to live whole lives. Men and women generally resolve the crisis of intimacy when they choose one another. From that moment on, in a situation of authentic conjugal chastity, all other options are existentially impossible because of the kingdom of love which has been established between them. So must the chaste celibate also spend his or her life resolving the crisis of intimacy "because of the kingdom". Then it may be said at Vatican III of our lives what Vatican II said about married love:

> Authentic *celibate* love is caught up into divine love and is directed and enriched by the redemptive power of Christ and the salvific action of the Church (see *Gaudium et Spes*, 48).

OBEDIENCE

As I introduced the question of chastity, I argued against the tendency to single out the vow of celibate chastity as the distinguishing mark of the Religious, claiming that it is important for us to retain the traditional term "chastity", as this kept the vowed life of the Religious firmly fixed within the universal call of all the baptised to chastity. Now, however, we must admit that there is one virtue in the Christian life which appears to touch and encompass the whole of the Christian response: obedience. In fact, there are ancient traditions of the Religious life in the Church where the only vow taken is obedience, as the rest is seen to follow logically from such a commitment. Because this is the case, obedience is certainly the most radically demanding of all the evangelical imperatives. Here we are touching the very heart of a Christian life and the reader may be somewhat overwhelmed by the idealistic nature of all that I am about to propose. Indeed, I am sensitive to the idealism of all that I have written so far, and I hesitate as I now find that the Gospel imperative of obedience almost leaves me breathless in the radical nature of its demands.

There is a wide gulf between the reality of the Christian life which we are attempting to live as individuals and in community, and the ideals of the evangelical imperatives. Nevertheless, we must not hesitate in our attempts, in the light of the Word of God, to find the ideal model against which and in the light of which we should continually examine our commitment to "the following of Christ as it is put before us in the Gospel" (*Perfectae Caritatis*, 2) The Word of God will never be accommodating. The prophet Jeremiah once spoke out in the name of Jahweh:

> Is not my word like fire, says the Lord,
> and like a hammer
> which breaks the rock in pieces? (Jer. 23,29)

The author of the letter to the Hebrews carries the imagery further. To the image of fire and hammer he adds that of a two-edged sword:

> The word of God is living and active,
> sharper than any two-edged sword,
> piercing into the division of soul, joints and marrow,
> and discerning the thoughts and intentions of the heart.
> (Heb. 4,12)

None of this is particularly comfortable. Precisely because our reflections are *biblical*, they are necessarily frighteningly idealistic, touching us at our deepest level and questioning us where we would prefer not to be questioned. The Word of God never apologises for its idealism. St. Paul did not write: "It *would be nice if* love were patient and kind; and *if love were not* jealous or boastful". On the contrary, he boldly proclaimed: "Love *is* patient and kind; love *is not* jealous or boastful" (I Cor. 13,4). I am also attempting to avoid the conditional, to present the biblical model as the imperative, idealistic though that imperative might be. As we turn now to examine the biblical model for Christian obedience and authority, this aspect of the Christian response may appear to be an almost impossible dream. Despite this fact, we must face the radical nature of the ideal to which we have been called, and to which we have responded in Baptism. If we are truly serious about the name we call ourselves, Christian, we must daily recommit ourselves to the imperatives of the Gospel of Jesus Christ in our ongoing decision to live on in a Christian community.

Despite the insistence of a long tradition in the Religious life, and my own indications above, that obedience encompassess all the Gospel values, it is surprising to find that there is no single text from the New Testament which has been consistently used in the tradition as biblical support for the vow and practice of obedience. We have already seen that discussions of poverty centred their attention on the Jerusalem community, as it is reported in the early chapters of the Acts of the Apostles, and also on the story of the rich young man, especially as it has been reported in Matt. 19,16-22. Chaste celibacy, it has long been argued, is based upon the eunuch saying in Matt. 19,12 and Paul's advice to the community at Corinth that they would do well to remain unmarried, so that they could devote all their energies and attention to the Lord. We have had reason, in the light of contemporary biblical scholarship, to question many of the traditional applications of those texts. Nevertheless, we have seen that they all retain their value, not as "proof texts", but as pointers to the authentic biblical background to the Christian and the Religious life: the radical commitment of the Christian and the Religious, in faith, to the following of Jesus of Nazareth. In other words, we should not regard special forms of life in the Church as being based on *one aspect* (or three aspects) of the Gospel demands. All Christians, and therefore all Religious, are called to live all the Gospel values in their entirety. *All* Christians are called to live *all* the Gospel, and the Religious life must be worked out within that view of things. As this is the case, then it is probably a helpful thing that none of these so-called "proof texts" are available for an immediate solution to the question of obedience, because, more than any of the vows, this is the one which is most biblical. This is the case because behind the call for obedience in the Christian life stands the call to follow the life-style of Jesus of Nazareth. We have already spent a great deal of time and space tracing the poverty and the chastity of Jesus in an attempt to find the prime model of Christian and Religious poverty and chastity. However, both of these aspects of Jesus' life pale into insignificance before the grandeur of his obedience.

Our study of Matt. 19,12 has already indicated that the chaste celibacy of Jesus flowed, as a necessary consequence, from another all-encompassing reality: the overpowering presence of the active lordship of God in his life. The same could be said for the poverty of Jesus. In my rapid portrait of Jesus' poverty, as it is reported in the Gospels (see above, p. 23), I argued that Jesus was to be seen as a man urgently pushing on to a God-determined destiny which left neither time nor opportunity for the gathering of possessions or the enjoyment of life's leisures. His life was dominated by a profound openness to God, whom he called his Father. As this is the case, I must spend some little time on the examination of the biblical background for all Christian obedience: the obedience of Jesus of Nazareth.

The Obedience of Jesus

I cannot hope to do justice to this central question within the limits of a few short pages. I merely wish to give some general indications of the centrality of obedience for a correct understanding of Jesus of Nazareth. We will see that the two basic questions about any man or woman, in the case of Jesus, will be answered in terms of obedience:

a) What did Jesus think he was doing?
b) Who did Jesus think he was?

The second question has to be answered through a discussion of:

i) Jesus as a Son
ii) Jesus as the Son of Man.

In many ways this study of the evangelical imperatives should have begun with the Christological synthesis which now follows. However, I was forced to wait till this stage, as it is only within the context of Jesus' obedience that the mystery of his life, his teaching and his paschal experience can be properly understood.

What did Jesus think he was doing?

There is a very short answer to this important question, as scholars are in universal agreement that Jesus of Nazareth saw his mission as the establishment of the kingdom of God among men and women. This theme is made very clear in Mark's Gospel, where the very first action described from the public ministry of Jesus is his urgent preaching:

> The time is fulfilled and the kingdom of God is at hand; repent and believe in the Gospel (Mark 1,15).

However, scholars do *not* agree on just what is meant by the "kingdom of God". In fact, Jesus and the evangelists after him seem to take it for granted that his listeners and their readers, respectively, would immediately recognise what the expression meant, as neither offer an explanation. One thing, nevertheless, is clear. Our English expression "the kingdom of God" does not do justice to the notion which seemed to dominate the preaching of Jesus, as our word "kingdom" is a rather static concept. It smacks of a territory with borders within which a certain king has authority. There do not appear to be any such limits in the kingdom which Jesus was preaching, and many scholars helpfully suggest that we would do better to speak of Jesus' announcing the "reign of God", with its more dynamic idea of God as king.

The idea of God as king is widely used in the Old Testament. He is king over the whole of creation, and especially in the lives of his human creation (see Pss. 22,28; 45,6; 103,19; 145,11. 13; Dan. 4,3. 34: I Chron. 17,14; 29,11). As king he saves, judges and loves his people, with whom he has established a covenant. The Old Testament idea of God as king also carries with it the idea of an end time, a "day of the Lord" which would spell the end of human history and the final manifestation of God's sovereign rule (see Is. 2,2-4; 24-27; Micah 4,1-4; Zech. 9-14). These notions would certainly have formed the general background for Jesus' proclamation of the reign of God, but with Jesus there was something extraordinarily different which cannot be explained in terms of the Old Testament notion of God's rule as king.

Despite the differences of opinion on what is exactly meant by Jesus' message of the reign of God, scholars come to their certainty about its all-important place in his preaching through the centrality of the notion in the parables of Jesus. Of all the material in the Gospels, we are in contact with the powerful yet simple preaching of Jesus of Nazareth in the parables. They were short and pungent, and they were printed indelibly in the minds and hearts of the first listeners to Jesus' own preaching. They were then faithfully passed on down through a generation, until they came to be recorded in the Gospels. Each evangelist, of course, uses them in his own way. This can be seen in the various "interpretations" which are added to the original parable (see, for example, Mark 4,13-20). Matthew, a writer with great sensitivity to Jewish ways of thought and expression, avoids the sacred name "God", and writes of "the kingdom of heaven". Nevertheless, the faithfulness of the evangelists to the original preaching of Jesus is very clear. There is a parable or a similitude to speak of all sorts of aspects of the reign of God among men and women:

> The Kingdom of God is as if a man should
> scatter seed upon the ground (Mark 4,26).
>
> With what can we compare the kingdom of God? . . .
> It is like a grain of mustard seed (Mark 4,30).
>
> The kingdom of heaven may be compared to a
> man who sowed good seed in his field (Matt. 13,24).
>
> The kingdom of heaven is like leaven which a
> woman took and hid in three measures of meal,
> till it was all leavened (Matt. 13,33).
>
> The kingdom of heaven is like a net which was
> thrown into the sea and gathered fish of
> every kind (Matt. 13,47).

The list could go on. I have merely used a series of similitudes which are found together in two famous collections of such material in Mark 4 and Matt. 13.

You will have noticed that I refer to both "parables" and "similitudes". Whereas once we tended to classify all of this Gospel material under the general name of "parable", modern scholars rightfully distinguish carefully between a similitude, which is a comparison: "The kingdom of God is as if . . ." and a parable, properly so called. A parable tells a story. It needs no introduction and goes straight to the point:

> There was a man who had two sons; and the younger of them said to his father . . . (Luke 15,11-12).
>
> Listen! A sower went out to sow. And as he
> sowed, some seed fell along the path, and
> the birds came . . . (Mark 4,3-4).
>
> There was a rich man who had a steward,
> and charges were brought to him that
> this man was wasting his goods (Luke 16,1).

However, be they similitudes or parables, the heart of Jesus' preaching can be touched here. While the similitude tends to instruct, the parable is much more challenging to the hearer or the reader. "It has been said, and with a great deal of truth, that the similitude *in*-forms, but a parable *re*-forms" (Jan Lambrecht). The power of the parabolic teaching of Jesus, in the strict sense, lies in the fact that a parable is incomplete until the reader has made some sort of response to it.

We cannot delay here to discuss all the details of the teaching of Jesus on the kingdom, but it should be clear that one of the unique things about Jesus of Nazareth was his burning conviction that the active reign of God had broken into the world, the hearts, the minds and the lives of men and women in his person, his activity — especially visible in his miraculous activity: "If it is by the finger of God that I cast out demons, then the kingdom of God has come upon you" (Luke 11,20), and in his preaching. The reign of God was already present, but not yet fulfilled, it brought peace, joy, harmony, but also challenges and responsibilities; it grows silently and swiftly, and is to be treasured beyond all treasures. Above all, it cannot be dismissed in its power to transform men and women.

What is most important, however, is that we grasp that for Jesus, the kingdom finally escaped all human categories. He could not even claim that it was *his* kingdom to give; it was the gift of God, his Father. By virtue of a unique relationship to the Father (see Matt. 11,25-27), Jesus claims a mysterious immediacy to God. He calls men to follow him (Mark 1,16-20), but the kingdom does not belong to Jesus, and its construction is not his work. It is the kingdom of his Father (Luke 12,32; 22,29-30) who alone knows the "hour" (Matt. 24,36). The kingdom of God "comes"; it can only be "received"; it must be prayed for (see Matt. 6,10; Mark 10,15; Luke 11,2). There seems to be a tension between God's kingship already being present in the person of Jesus, and yet it is still to come. These paradoxes, and the seeming contradictions which abound in the parables and the teaching about the kingdom simply indicate the sovereign freedom of God's intervention. This is particularly clear in one of the major discussions about the parables of the kingdom. Scholars have been baffled by the question of when it is or will be finally established. There have been many theories and none of them is entirely satisfactory. It *must* be this way, because there can be no human "system" which can hope to describe the kingdom, as Jesus preached it. The sayings about the kingdom and the parables cannot be brought into total harmony: some sayings indicate a fixed period of time (see Matt. 10,23; Mark 9,1; 13,30), while others reject all attempts to fix a date (see Mark 13,32); some parables speak of growth (see Mark 4; Matt. 13,24-30), while others speak of "entering" a kingdom already established (see Luke 13,24; Matt. 7,13). This is due to the nature of the kingdom of God as it was preached by Jesus. It is an event which rounds off history definitively, and thus is constantly present in every single situation as it moves towards that consummation. Realities within history can only very improperly be signs of the kingdom of God, no matter how full of meaning they might be. The kingdom escapes the grasp of human science and systems. It is basic to the message of Jesus that the world and its situation can only be understood in the light of God's kingship, but the kingship of God can never be seen as simply a projection of anything of this world. If this is correct, we can understand why Jesus, and the evangelists who followed his teaching, never attempted to describe just what he meant by his expression "the kingdom of God". He necessarily spoke in parables (see Mark 4,33-34), similes, summonses and maxims which gave hints of a transcendent reality. Ultimately, the kingdom preached by Jesus turns the world and the values of the world upside down. It is the world shattering, counter-cultural promise of God's loving gift to a struggling humanity.

Finally, Jesus not only *preached* such parables. He lived them. To push this further, we must say that the kingdom of God is intimately associated with — not only what he said — but with what he did: the sharing of his table with sinners, the peace of his own person, the real chance of conversion offered to sinners, and above all, his death on the cross. To exemplify this, I would like to offer you a sample interpretation of the parable of the father with two sons (commonly, and erroneously, called the parable of the prodigal son: Luke 15,11-32). I am taking this interpretation from a powerful little book published recently by Eduard Schweizer, *Luke: A Challenge to Present Theology* (Atlanta, John Knox Press, 1982) pp. 80-81. There is no need for me to repeat the story; you all know it well. I would like to show, as a conclusion to these brief reflections on what Jesus thought he was doing, the implications of this parable.

The most surprising fact of this story is the attitude of this father who does not want to dominate, to subject his sons to his own will. The story of the two sons seems to run down to the end in a well-known psychological pattern. But in the parable of Jesus, the father butts in. He does not want to possess his sons. In an incredible way he leads them to total freedom, which the younger son finds in the home of the father and which the elder son should also find there. The father does not even preach a sermon or wait for a confession of sins. On the contrary, he cuts it short in the case of the younger son, and he accepts his elder one without reserve: "Son, you are always with me and all that is mine is yours". There is no word to the younger son, only the act of welcome, and there is but a word of affirmation to the elder one. What this father demonstrates with his acts is rather more like a sacramental manifestation of an incredible love than like preaching.

Jesus has not merely told this parable. He has lived it. Perhaps only a month or two later he is hanging on the cross, people shouting at him: "Descend from the cross and we shall believe in you". Is this the almighty God? Jesus could have prayed and his father would have sent him more than twelve legions of angels (Matt. 26,53). And yet he is totally powerless, because he has decided to love. Therefore he has nothing, not even a square inch of land to stay upon, not even the freedom to move his hand or foot an inch to the left or to the right. Nailed securely on solid wood, separated from the earth on which he was living, he is hanging there in total powerlessness. He has nothing more than his heart full of love and a few last words by which he invites the people around him to join him and to come to the banquet hall of the father.

It is Jesus who has told *and* lived the parable of the powerless almighty father, Jesus who knows his father in heaven better than anyone else knows him. Should it not be true that this his father in heaven is to be found, first of all, where the father stands at the end of the parable — out in the dark where the rebels are fighting against him.

Jesus the teller of parables and Jesus who *is* the parable rocks the world to its foundations in two ways:

a) He reveals a different sort of God to the one expected and invented by the religions and culture of his own day. The parable retains its power today, because the God revealed by Jesus then is as much a surprise to us all now as he was then.

b) Jesus "lives" the parable. In a unique way, therefore, he has revealed God's presence, God's active reign among men and women in word and in deed ... in his very person. God is present in Jesus of Nazareth.

If this is what Jesus of Nazareth claimed to bring in his person, through the parable of his own life, then the question which must be asked, and all too rapidly answered, is the question that his contemporaries were all asking: "Who does this man think he is?" (see for example, Mark 1,27;2,7; 4,41; 6,2; John 12,34). According to the Gospels, he understood himself as a Son and as the Son of Man.

Jesus as a Son

We must take care in our approach to this question, remembering that we are concerned with Jesus' own idea of himself. Clearly, the idea of Jesus as "Son" and "Son of God" stands at the centre of the christological belief of the confessing Christian Church. Already in the earliest strata of the New Testament we find a confession of faith in Jesus as "Son". It is widely believed that the opening verses of the letter to the Romans was a very early confession of faith which Paul used for his own purposes:

> The gospel concerning his Son
> who was born of the seed of David
> according to the flesh
> but was constituted Son of God in power
> according to the spirit of holiness
> by resurrection from the dead,
> Jesus Christ our Lord (Rom. 1,3-4).

The Gospels also carry the same belief, even though each evangelist will have his different approach to Jesus' sonship. It forms a sort of framework for the earliest of the Gospels, coming at the beginning (Mark 1,1. 11), the centre (9,7) and at the end of Mark's story (15,39). By the time the Fourth Gospel finally appeared (about 100) faith in Jesus of Nazareth as "the Son" had become the christological category which dominated this Gospel's Christology. The theological structure of the Fourth Gospel is incomprehensible unless one sees the centrality of the God-Jesus relationship in terms of Father-Son. It would be pointless to list all the passages which show this, and the Fourth Evangelist tells us himself just what it meant to him when he concludes his Gospel by telling his readers why he wrote it:

> These things are written that you may go on
> believing that Jesus is the Christ, the
> Son of God, and that believing you may have
> life in his name (John 20,31. A.T. See also 3,16-21
> and 5,19-30).

We have already seen, however, that the documents of the New Testament are a profound confession of faith, very often conditioned in their expression by the pastoral situation into which they were directed, as well as by the particular faith experience and vision of the person or persons responsible for the document. They do not claim to be objective records of what actually happened during the earthly days of Jesus, as they have been written entirely in the blinding light of the resurrection and in the Spirit of the Risen Lord in their midst. Our passage from Romans already shows this: "constituted Son of God in power . . . by resurrection from the dead" (Rom. 1,4). The Fourth Evangelist also makes no secret of the fact that it was the Risen Lord who brought true faith and understanding to the early Church:

> His disciples did not understand this at first;
> but when Jesus was glorified,
> then they remembered that this had been written of him
> and had been done to him (John 12,16. See the same
> sentiments in 2,22).

The developing consciousness of Jesus' sonship and its expression in the New Testament are clearly a post-resurrectional, Spirit-filled growth in faith and understanding. Of course, expressions of faith in Jesus as "Son" and "the Son of God" did not cease with the Fourth Gospel. They were the major christological categories used at the early Councils of Nicaea (325) and Chalcedon (451) in their attempt to deal with the difficult theological divisions which were tearing the Church apart at that time. Naturally, our understanding of Jesus is largely determined by what these Councils taught, but "doctrine should not determine interpretation; rather should interpretation undergird doctrine" (John Marsh). We are attempting to rediscover how Jesus himself lived his sonship.

To understand fully Jesus' uniqueness, it is important to know that Old Testament Judaism already had a two-fold use of the title "son of God". First, there was an application of the title to individual persons. We find it applied three times to a king. God says of Solomon: "I will be his father, and he shall be my son" (II Sam. 7,14). In Ps. 2,7 there is a clear application of the title to a king at his enthronement: "You are my son, this day I become your father". The same imagery is found in Ps. 89,26-29. Notice that there is no idea of God's "begetting" a son, but the son is adopted. For Jewish thought this meant that the king was to function, to rule as an adopted son of God, and this meant that he would live by and rule by the commandments of God. The second use of the term "son of God" found in the Old Testament is its application to the people as a whole. Moses was told to say to Pharoah that "Israel is my first born son" (Exod. 4,22). The people can cry out: "Thou, O Lord art our father (Is. 63,16) and Hosea can recall, "When Israel was a child, I loved him, and out of Egypt I called my son" (Hosea 11,1. See Deut. 1,31; 32,6-7). Again, however, this widespread notion (see further Deut. 14,1; 18,5; 32,18; Is. 43,6; 63,8; Jer. 3,4; 19,22; 31,9; Pss. 34,11; 82,6; 149,2) never has the idea of a physical fatherhood or sonship; it means that Israel, if it were to be regarded as God's people, was to be totally dependent and subordinate to Jahweh.

Jesus, of course, would have been formed in that tradition. Deeply caught up in God's history of salvation through his chosen people, he too would have been caught up in the idea of that faithful people as a "son of God", totally dependent and subordinate to Jahweh. However, this is not enough. There is something more, something unique about Jesus of Nazareth which set him apart from the other "sons of God". The key to that uniqueness is to be found in his use of the term *abba* to speak, in prayer, directly to the God of Israel. All of the Gospels, and especially Luke's Gospel, present Jesus as a man who prayed to God regularly. In his prayer Jesus regularly addresses God as "Father" (Greek: *pater*. See, for example, Matt. 11,25-27 and John 17). On one occasion, however, the Evangelist Mark does not translate the Aramaic term which Jesus would have used. Not only do we have here a precious testimony of the term which Jesus used to speak to Jahweh in prayer, but the contents of the prayer itself can be regarded as a synthesis of what it means to call Jahweh *abba*:

> Abba, Father, all things are possible to thee;
> remove this cup from me;
> yet not what I will but what thou wilt (Mark 14,36).

The expression *abba* could have only come into the Gospel tradition because Jesus used it . . . and because he used it regularly. We have already seen that the use of the term "eunuch" crept into the Gospel traditions because Jesus used it. It is still to be found in the Gospels, despite its outrageous connotations, because Jesus himself said it, and because he said it regularly. The same must be said for the term *abba*, even though in this case the outrageous nature of the term arises from quite a different background. The ordinary word for "father" in Aramaic and Hebrew is *ab*. The addition of a diminutive to form *abba* is only possible within the context of a union of deep intimacy and affection between father and child. It is often paralleled with the English "daddy", but this is not accurate. Such an expression in English drops out of usage as a child matures. This is not the case with *abba*. The expression in Aramaic/Hebrew reflects *the quality of a relationship*, and thus does not fade as a son or daughter matures. Within a Jewish world where reverence for Jahweh had reached such extremes that "the name" could not even be pronounced, we find this extraordinary form of address on the lips of Jesus: *abba*.

Never before had anyone dared to speak to the God of Israel in such endearing and close terms. It appears that it was a regular form of prayer for Jesus, even though it is only found expressly in Mark 14,36. The many other places in the Gospels where Jesus speaks to God as "Father" are probably a translation into Greek (*pater*) of what was originally the endearing and deeply personal Aramaic word on the lips of Jesus of Nazareth: *abba*. A further indication that the term comes from Jesus himself is found in the fact that it was immediately picked up and freely used in the prayers of his followers (see Matt. 6,9; Luke 11,2; Rom. 8,15; Gal. 4,6). The earliest Christians could speak to God in this daringly fresh way because Jesus had done so before them.

All this evidence points to a very important consideration about Jesus' understanding of himself. He clearly saw himself as related to the God of Israel in terms of an obedient and loving son. This throws further light on the urgency behind the life of Jesus which can be found behind all the Gospel portraits of Jesus: an urgency to go on into a future into which, he believed, God his Father was leading him. All Jesus could do was respond radically, without ever swerving from the will and plan of God, his Father. Thus, we can conclude, the historical Jesus lived out a life of sonship in terms of a complete, unswerving and radical obedience, cost what it may. This whole mystery has been magnificently synthesised by the author of the letter to the Hebrews:

> In the days of his flesh, Jesus offered up
> prayers and supplications, with loud cries and tears,
> to him who was able to save him from death, and he
> was heard for his godly fear. Although he was a Son,
> he learned obedience through suffering (Heb. 5,7-8).

Now we are in a better position to understand the extraordinarily bold and radically new teaching of Jesus which we examined in our rapid analysis of his teaching on the kingdom. We saw there that Jesus spoke out of a mysterious immediacy with God, and his teaching raised the question of who he might be to speak with such authority. Here we have a large part of the answer: a son radically open in obedience to the God of Israel. In other words, we can only understand who Jesus was in terms of his obedience, and we can only understand his preaching of the kingdom as a consequence of such obedience. We have already seen in our glance at the parable of the father and the two sons (Luke 15,11-32) that Jesus not only *teaches* parables, but that he *is* that parable. This indicates that his obedience led him to preach and to live the presence of God's active reign among men and women, *cost what it may.* Just what did it cost him? This must be explained in terms of Jesus' own understanding of himself as "the Son of Man".

Jesus as the Son of Man

Jesus calls himself "the Son of Man" over seventy times in the Gospels. Although many of these are parallels, where Matthew and Luke are merely repeating what they found in Mark or in their common source, this strange term is used more than any other to speak of Jesus. What is even more extraordinary and important is the fact that *only* Jesus uses it, and he always uses it to speak of himself. No other person in the Gospels is called "the Son of Man", and no one else ever addresses Jesus as "the Son of Man" (John 12,34 is really no exception to this). It would appear that we have here the key to what Jesus thought about himself. Right or wrong, if a person consistently gives himself a title, then that person must think it describes his person and activity. What, then, does the term "the Son of Man" mean?

It is at this stage that difficulties begin to appear. Some would say that the expression meant nothing more than "I" on the lips of Jesus, and that the way in which it is used in the Gospels was a christological development which took place in the later Church. It is found, however, in Dan. 7,13, and it appears to me that this was the source of Jesus' use of the term. It is so central to our understanding of Jesus that I would like to offer a brief analysis of that famous chapter.

The Book of Daniel was written about 165 B.C., during

the terrible persecutions inflicted upon the faithful ones in Israel by the Hellenistic king, Antiochus IV of Syria. In the fashion of Alexander the Great of Macedonia (died in 323 B.C.), the great Hellenistic kings attempted to impose their religion and culture upon all their subjects. Antiochus IV, who ruled in Syria from 175 till 163 B.C., pursued this policy with great vigour. The gruesome stories of suffering and martyrdom found in the Books of the Maccabees (see above, pp. 20-21) come from the same period. It is very important, for a correct understanding of the term "son of man" in Dan. 7,13, to appreciate that the Book of Daniel was written to a suffering people who really had little or no hope of ever finding a human solution to the agonies which their faith in Jahweh was creating for them. The response of the Maccabees to such suffering was military, while the response of the author of the Book of Daniel was religious. He uses a difficult form of literature (called "apocalyptic") in which strange language and images are used to convey his basic belief: in the end, over against all evil and suffering, God will eventually have the final word. This sort of message is widely found in Jewish literature of that period. It was written to exhort a suffering people in a seemingly hopeless human situation to remain faithful to their God. He would ultimately be victorious over the wicked oppressors of his faithful ones (Daniel calls them his "holy ones". See Dan. 7,18. 22. 25. 27). The author of the Book of Daniel argues this case with particular force in Dan. 7.

The reader is told of a vision in the night (7,1-2) in which Daniel sees four great beasts, each one more terrible than the other, leading to the fourth, most horrific of all. These beasts represent the persecutors of Israel.

— Babylon: "like a lion and had eagles' wings" (v. 4).
— the Medes: "like a bear . . . raised up on one side; it had three ribs in its mouth . . . and it was told 'Devour much flesh'" (v. 5).
— Persia: "like a leopard with four wings of a bird on its back; and the beast had four heads; and dominion was given to it" (v. 6).

— Last, and most terrible of all, the Hellenistic empire, the present persecution: "a fourth beast, terrible and dreadful and exceedingly strong; and it had great iron teeth; it devoured and broke in pieces, and stamped the residue with its feet" (v. 7).

Antiochus IV himself is identified (see v. 8: a small, arrogant horn which plucked out three of the original horns to take their place: a reference to the three violent deaths necessary for Antiochus to take control in Syria).

The scene is dark indeed. Animal violence gathers, and this was the lived experience of Israel in 165 B.C. However, the solution to the problem is at hand; it is to be found in the ultimate authority of God. The vision changes:

> As I looked
> thrones were placed
> and one that was ancient of days
> took his seat . . .
> the court sat in judgment,
> and the books were opened (vv. 9-10).

The three former persecutors lose all their power (v. 12) and the fourth "beast was slain, and its body destroyed and given over to be burned with fire" (v. 11).

> And behold with the clouds of heaven
> there came *one like a son of man*
> and he came to the Ancient of Days
> and was presented before him.
> And to him was given dominion
> and glory and kingdom . . .
> His dominion is an everlasting dominion,
> which shall not pass away
> and his kingdom one
> that shall not be destroyed (vv. 13-14).

The rest of the chapter (vv. 15-28) is devoted to an explanation of the dream, and there the term "son of man" does not appear. It is replaced by the expression "the saints (the holy ones) of the Most High" (vv. 18, 22. 25. 27) as the interpretation of the dream tells the story of a persecuted people who place their trust and hope in the ultimate victory of God:

> And the kingdom and the dominion
> and the greatness of the kingdoms
> under the whole heaven
> shall be given to the people of
> *the saints of the Most High*;
> their kingdom shall be an everlasting kingdom,
> and all dominions shall serve and obey them (v. 27).

Clearly the "one like a son of man" (in v. 13, over against all the "animal-like" figures of those opposed to God and his people) is an individualisation and personification of a suffering people, "the saints of the Most High" who are promised, in the midst of their suffering, that in the end they will have the last word through the saving action of their God.

This is where Jesus of Nazareth found his strange title, but when he came to take it over, he no longer spoke of "a son of man". He applied it to himself as "*the* Son of Man". Like the holy ones in Israel in Dan. 7, Jesus saw that his life-style was leading him into suffering, persecution and death. This was the only way which he could possibly go. The radical and disturbing nature of the kingdom he preached, over against the accepted "kingdoms" of both Jewish and Roman authority and the unique immediacy to God which was so obvious in the authority behind all that he said and did could not go unchecked. It was too dangerous. Then, he was gathering a following, a group of people who were prepared to abandon the "old ways" to follow the way of Jesus of Nazareth. He had to be stopped, and Jesus himself would have been very aware that such processes were in motion. The very quality of his life, therefore, led him into conflict, suffering and ultimately death at the hands of the powers of this world. Yet, by taking over the term "the Son of Man" he announced that his way of suffering, persecution and loss of self in love and service was not senseless. In fact, it gave sense and purpose to his whole life. Using a familiar term "son of man" and pointing to himself as "the Son of Man" Jesus showed and taught that he was going further and further away from all human success, away from what *he* might desire (see Mark 14,36 again), into a mysterious future which he could not determine, full of trust, hope, love and obedience to the God of Israel, whom he called *abba.* How was such an attitude of loss of self in love and service possible? It was precisely because of his relationship of obedience as "Son" that his experience as "the Son of Man" made sense. He went on, not *knowing* all the details of what might stand before him, but in his obedience, *trusting* that, no matter what came his way, God his Father would have the last word. And that was exactly how it happened: a death, yes; but followed by the saving and glorious intervention of God in the resurrection. Jesus, Son of God and Son of Man is at the one time the most obedient and the most free human being that ever existed. He had no desire or need to *control* his future, as his radical openness and trust in his Father freed him from all such concerns.

Here we have a Jesus we can follow. He was completely open to his Father in obedience, and that obedience gave him the freedom which led him away from himself into the strange loss of himself in love: an obedient suffering love that ultimately made sense in the resurrection. Now it becomes clear that only in Jesus has the kingdom been definitively present. As I have already mentioned, Jesus not only preaches the parables of the kingdom, Jesus *is* the parable of the kingdom. This is the way that all Christians are asked to go when they are asked to "walk behind Jesus of Nazareth". Jesus has done it, and he has thus become the first-born from the death and slavery that sin and the desire to control the world have brought. Those who are prepared to follow Jesus, Son and Son of Man, will follow him right through to the ultimate freedom that only resurrection and the definitive establishment of the rule of God in our lives can give. Only now can we begin to sense the centrality of obedience in the life of a Christian, a follower of the obedient Christ.

Vatican II

When the Second Vatican Council came to reflect upon the vowed form of obedience in the Religious life they saw that the attitude of Jesus had to be central to any Conciliar statement (*Perfectae Caritatis*, 14). It is again interesting to notice that the document is formulated in rather traditional language which needs careful interpretation, as there are several expressions contained within it which contemporary Religious and contemporary theologies of the Religious life would find very awkward. It is important to see that, despite some of the *language* used, the traditional *idea* behind this statement still has a fundamental importance and application to our contemporary scene.

The document from the Council opens with an unfortunate choice of terms which could cause difficulty:

> By their profession of obedience, religious offer the full dedication of their own wills as a sacrifice of themselves to God, and by this means they are united more permanently and securely with God's saving will (*Perfectae Caritatis*, 14).

The difficulties which arise from such a statement stem from two basic issues:

a) The first part of the statement gives the impression that obedience in the Religious life means that there is no further opportunity to exercise one's own will. To offer one's own will as a sacrifice could be taken to mean that one no longer has a will of one's own! Such a position —somewhat reminiscent of an older concept in the asceticism of the Religious life (often spoken about but, fortunately, seldom practised) — is theologically indefensible. God did not create men and women with all their uniqueness so that they could "sacrifice" that uniqueness. We must apply to these considerations what we have already gleaned from our analysis of *Gaudium et Spes*, 36: men and women are not saved *despite* their belonging to the world of material things, *despite* the fact that they are flesh and blood, and therefore led by their heart and their mind, working together in a God-directed, but free, will, but *because of all these things.* We are called to work out our salvation through an enthusiastic and positive response to God in Christ Jesus in and through our being situated in God's creation. Any theology of obedience which attempts to lift men and women out of that situation must be a false one, and will inevitably lead to frustration.

b) The second major affirmation which this opening statement makes is that through the practice of obedience, Religious have a means to a *more* permanent and secure unity with God's will. Once again we find the tendency to present the Religious state as a "better" form of life within the Church. As I have insisted *ad nauseam* through these pages, this tradition — although much respected and defended — does not form part of the biblical message on holiness, and runs contrary to what the Council itself taught in *Lumen Gentium*, 40.

The Council document then proceeds to describe the biblical background for obedience in the Religious life:

> After the example of Jesus Christ, who came to do his Father's will (cf Jn. 4,34; 5,30; Heb. 10,7; Ps. 39,9) and "taking the form of a servant" (Phil. 2,7) learned obedience through what he suffered (Heb. 10,8), religious moved by the Holy Spirit subject themselves in faith to those who hold God's place, their superiors.

As we have already seen from our short portrait of the obedience of Jesus, the Council Fathers have placed their finger on what is, ultimately, the only motivation for obedience within the Christian view of things: the obedience of Jesus Christ. In fact, the two texts which are explicitly cited (Phil. 2,7 and Heb. 10,8) probably represent the best synthesis of the Gospel portrait of the obedience of Jesus. However, what of the reference to the superiors as "those who hold God's place"? Again we find ourselves faced with what could be regarded as traditional language reflecting an outmoded view. However, one must be careful not to dismiss what is being said here. If such an expression means that a superior, purely by grace of his or her authority, suddenly takes on plenipotentiary powers, then this would be an outrageous claim. It appears to me, nevertheless, that there is possibly a more profoundly biblical idea behind the expression, but more will be said of that below.

Picking up the reference to superiors, the Council document then proceeds — again on the basis of the experience of Jesus — to show how obedience naturally flows into mission.

> Through them (superiors) they are led to serve all their brothers in Christ, just as Christ ministered to his brothers in submission to the Father and laid down his life for the redemption of many (cf Matt. 20,28; 10,14-18). Thus they are bound more closely to the Church's service as they endeavour to attain to the measure of the stature of the fulness of Christ (cf Eph. 4,13).

This is a fine reflection, and the reader will have sensed how beautifully and how accurately the experience of Jesus of Nazareth has been transferred into the experience of the obedient Religious. Once again we find the use of a "more" expression. The document claims that, through obedience, the Religious is "bound more closely to the Church's service". This time, however, there is no difficulty. The Religious can certainly lay claim to a closer association with the public ministry of the Church. The document — at this stage — does not indicate that such a role makes the Religious "better". On the contrary, there is that fine indication that through their particular association with the Church's service "they endeavour to attain " the perfection of love — the vocation of all Christians (*Lumen Gentium*, 40) — here expressed in terms of "the stature of the fullness of Christ".

Thus, even though we find some of the older, unsatisfactory, expressions in this Conciliar statement, also present is an all-important biblical model, insisting that the Religious, in publicly professing obedience, is called to follow the life-style of Jesus of Nazareth. The two-fold dimension of such a life-style is beautifully described: an openness to God which leads to a preparedness to lay one's life on the line "for the redemption of many". But once we have established that the imitation of Jesus of Nazareth is where our obedience has its source, then we can see that my continual insistence throughout this book again comes to the fore: such a demand cannot be regarded as an evangelical *counsel.* It must be an imperative. If, as *Perfectae Caritatis,* 14 so rightly insists, a Religious must be obedient in imitation of Christ, then *all Christians* must be obedient, in some way. The Religious is not the only one who has been called to imitate Christ. All the baptised have committed themselves to such a life-style. This must be kept in mind as I now turn to examine how the Religious should respond to his or her vocation to a certain *form* of obedience within the universal call of all the baptised to follow the way of Jesus of Nazareth.

Obedience: The Imitation of Christ

Any Religious community should be a microcosm of the Church: the Church in action, a visible, tangible group attempting to live publicly and prophetically what the Christian Church was instituted to be: a sign and bearer of God's uniting hope, love and salvation to the whole world. It exists because the people who make up that community believe in the salvation which comes to us, in the Church, through Jesus Christ, the unique bringer of the active reign of God among men and women, Son of God and Son of Man. We have not come together as members of an economic community, a sporting group, a social group, or any other form of "community". The Church, and *a fortiori* a Religious community, is a *faith* community. We have come together because of an experience of the risen Lord in our lives, an experience of faith, and the goal of each one of us is to repeat in our lives the life of the person who has touched us in our commitment of faith, to imitate the object of our faith as closely as possible — or to spend the rest of our lives working at it anyway! The immensity of that challenge can be gathered from the few pages which I have dedicated to my short portrait of the person of Jesus of Nazareth.

The fundamental need, therefore, of a Religious committed publicly to this life-style through a vow taken in the Church and before the world, is to know Jesus of Nazareth. How can one imitate a person if one does not know him? This, I feel, is one of the great problems of the Church, and thus of the Religious life. A recognition of the problem stands behind the Council's insistence that renewal of the Religious life take the following of Jesus, as he is put before us in the Gospels, as one of its major criteria (see *Perfectae Caritatis*, 2). We hear so often: "Be close to Jesus", "Know Jesus", "Imitate Jesus", "Pray as Jesus prayed", "Love as Jesus loved". But who is he? What does he mean to me? Does he remain that image which appealed to me as a teenager? Have I grown in my understanding of the person and the personality of this man? These are vitally important questions which are often never posed. We must *know* Christ Jesus, and not just commit ourselves to some fantasy, or some attractive artistic presentation of him which strikes our fancy, but which can always be kept in a frame on a wall. Such an attitude can be "pretty", but it is shallow and superficial. A shallow, false, fanciful or unrealistic Christology *necessarily* produces a false, fanciful or unrealistic Christianity. This sort of Christology generally falls back upon an authoritarian Ecclesiology to stay alive. One generally finds that people who are not deeply immersed in the rediscovery of Jesus and the quality of his life in their own journey through history move quickly to see their "faith" as one lived in a complete and uncritical acceptance of anything that is uttered by the upper echelons of the hierarchy. This is not sufficient, as the Christian is called to know Christ Jesus, and to move further and further away from our own securities into God's future, cost what it may. As should be obvious from my sketch of the obedience of Jesus of Nazareth, this is the only way that a knowledge of Christ can possibly lead us. The more we grow in our Christianity, the more we will be prepared to cast off *our* ideas so that we might lose ourselves in the mystery of the following of Jesus of Nazareth, Son and Son of Man. This is a life of faith, and it is the reason why we exist as a Church, and as a Religious community.

The challenge of faith, however, must become real and vital, but this will only happen when it becomes a *personal* challenge. Only when we are called into action, or into a quality of life through the impact of a personalty upon us will the challenge really transform us. Too often faith is seen as a commitment to an ideology, a commitment to a set of values, a certain form of Law, of worship, of Church structure and organisation. All of these things have their place, but they must be the consequences of a prior and all-encompassing commitment to a *person.* Unless the challenge of faith is real and personal, it becomes either a pious chasing after rainbows or an arid commitment to the more external and formal elements of a "Church".

This was immediately recognised in the early Church. The earliest records we have of Christian communities are the letters of Paul and, as we will see, his whole theology of obedience and authority rests upon the premise of the *personal* challenge to a life of faith. A document which is a great synthesis of many of his major ideas demands of the Ephesians: "Be imitators of God as beloved children" (Eph. 5,1). Such a notion would not be new to a community familiar with Jewish thought, as we have already seen. It was a rather common idea in the Old Testament that the perfect Israel was a "son of God", and that this could be embodied in the person of the king, whose perfect observance of God's will and ways would make him God's son. In other words, to imitate God as a child would imitate a father is a perfectly good Old Testament way of speaking of holiness. But our author goes further, and speaks in more detail of the modality of such an imitation:

> And walk in love,
> as Christ loved us and gave himself up for us,
> a fragrant offering and sacrifice to God (Eph. 5,1-2).

To be an imitator of God in the traditional Old Testament sense sounds attractive enough, but how is this done? The Ephesians are told, in a first moment, that it is only possible through walking in love. Now, at least, they have something a little more concrete, but there are all sorts of activities called — rightly or wrongly — by the name of "love". Is there any further indication of how the Christian should love? A definite concrete model is offered: "as Christ loved us". The Church is no longer only challenged with a God who is always present yet never totally available, a God who reveals himself through battles, prophets, words, through times of plenty and times of famine. That was the Old Testament's preparation for the Christ event, in its magnificent yet mystery-filled understanding of Jahweh. Now he has become a personal encounter with a concrete historical figure called Jesus of Nazareth, and the Ephesians are told that they must imitate the way he loved. Jesus is the concrete example; to imitate God, Christians have to love as Christ loved, that is, completely, in a radical obedience to God our Father.

However, even a slight knowledge of this community reveals another problem. How many people in Ephesus knew Jesus? For how many people in Ephesus did that appeal to Jesus and his gift of self in love represent a personal calling? Probably no one. Paul, the Apostle of the Gentiles, would have faced this situation in almost all of his communities. On the one hand he saw the imitation of Christ as essential to Christian life, but on the other he was preaching this message to a people who had only *heard of* Jesus Christ. Thus Paul had to somehow render historical the Christ-Christian challenge. Paul was a realist; he was aware that one can talk on endlessly about a great figure from the past, and even about the greatness of his loving, but if his love is such that it still catches up the Christian and challenges him or her to a quality of life, then it must become a personal challenge, and not just something that one talks about. Words and ideas can quickly cheapen and can easily be forced into differing moulds, but the quality of a life can survive all of this. Thus, to maintain in his communities the challenge of the quality of the life of Jesus, Paul took the only step possible, and in so doing he laid the theological basis for all subsequent Christian authority:

> Be imitators of me, as I am of Christ (I Cor. 11,1).

Paul presents himself as an historical, concrete presence in the community who demands obedience from them on the basis of the fact that he is presenting the demands of the life-style of Jesus Christ to them. This extraordinary statement from Paul: "Be imitators of me, as I am of Christ", has sometimes been explained away as an example of Paul's possible arrogance; Paul in a weak moment, when he has become a little "big-headed", anxious to let his community know of his dignity and importance. However, all the letters of Paul which he wrote to communities which knew him personally contain similar statements (see I Thess. 1,6; I Cor. 4,16-17; Gal. 4,12; Phil. 4,9). It would have been unrealistic of Paul to write to the Romans or to the Colossians, whom he had never met: "Be imitators of me ..." because they did not know him as a physical, historical imitator of Christ in their midst.

In fact, this idea is not restricted to the Pauline writings. The first letter of Peter contains something very similar. Addressing himself to the leaders of the community the author writes:

> Tend the flock of God that is in your charge not by constraint but willingly, not for shameful gain but eagerly, not as domineering over those in your charge but by being an example to the flock. An example that merits imitation (I Peter 5,2-3).

As with Paul, the author is insisting that authority is only to be had and exercised by one who "willingly" and "eagerly" is prepared to lead his flock by example, by the quality of his or her own life, repeating in history the quality of the life of Jesus of Nazareth.

Paul's awareness that it was useless merely to "preach" Christ is shown by the fact that he keeps coming back to this principle each time he writes to one of the communities which has known him "in the flesh". He himself knows that the only way that he can claim to have any authority in these early Christian communities is by insisting that he represents the very presence of Christ in their midst. Even though the explicit expression "Be imitators of me ..." is not found, perhaps the clearest example of his position on this comes at the end of the first chapter of the letter to his beloved community at Philippi:

> For me to live is Christ and to die is gain. If it is to be life in the flesh, that means fruitful labour for me. Yet which I shall choose I cannot tell. I am hard pressed between the two. My desire is to depart and be with Christ, for that is far better. But to remain *in the flesh* is more necessary on your account. Convinced of this I know that I shall remain and continue with you all, for your progress and joy in the faith, so that *in me* you may have ample cause to glory *in Christ Jesus*, because of my coming to you again (Phil. 1,21-26).

The choice which Paul suggests that he has to make is a rhetorical device, as he has no authority to decide whether he shall live or die. This device, however, is skilfully used to throw into strong relief the need for a "fleshly" historical presence of the man Paul in the community at Philippi, so that they may find again the challenge of the person and message of Jesus of Nazareth. The pastoral presence of Paul in his community is not merely as a teacher, a man of *words*. The Philippians are to find in his very flesh and blood presence among them the presence of the challenge of the life and love of Jesus of Nazareth: "*in me* you may have ample cause to glory *in Christ Jesus*".

This Pauline solution to the problem of obedience and authority in a Christian community is something which must go on down through the ages. A little reflection will show that it is the *only* way in which we can hope to have valid authority in a Christian community. As I have already insisted, we do not belong to economic communities, sporting or social groups ... or any other form of *secular* community structure. We belong to a faith community. How often errors are made here. There has been a great post-Conciliar movement to democratise the Religious life, but what is the guarantee that "democracy" is what is needed? Democracy is a form of government invented by the Greeks in the fifth century B.C. It may well work for us . . . but it must not become a new "absolute". Like any other "system" of government, it is a man-made system and will consequently never provide all the answers for a community which has gathered together because of a shared faith in Christ Jesus. Our post-Conciliar experiments have already shown us that. Similarly, how often we have heard it said over the chaos of some recent situations: "If you were working in a bank and you were told to do such and such, then you would have to do it". The answer is near at hand, of course: "I am not working in a bank. I belong to a faith community that has its sense and unity because of our shared faith in Christ Jesus". It is from this basic *raison d'être* of our communities that we must work out our theology of obedience, and any "system" which allows this to work, which throws into relief the challenge of the life-style of the obedient Jesus of Nazareth, will be satisfactory. Any other foundation would be false. Our Christian and Religious communities are based on the Incarnation. This is ultimately the root cause of Paul's insistence that his "fleshly" historical presence in his community is all-important for their finding and following of Jesus. I cannot stress this enough because it is here that, despite the somewhat traditional language used by the Council Fathers, the teaching of *Perfectae Caritatis*, 14 finds its theological basis.

The statement from the Council spoke of the superior's taking the place of God. I would find that impossible to accept if it meant that the superior was God on earth, with plenipotentiary powers over all men. It is not that the superior has a "hot line" to God, but that the authority figure renders "incarnational", in a historical, flesh and blood man or woman, the call to be imitators of Christ. The Christian authority-figure has authority as he or she can repeat with Paul:

Be imitators of me, as I am of Christ!

What is being presented here as the ideal is not a new notion in the history of the Religious life. It stands at the heart of St. Benedict's treatment of "What kind of man the Abbot ought to be" in his Rule (drawn up in about 540). He wrote: "He is believed to hold the place of Christ in the monastery", and later he added: "He should show forth all goodness and holiness by his deeds rather than his words" (*The Rule of St. Benedict*, chapter 2). It is also interesting, in the light of our short reflection upon the obedience of Jesus, that the word "abbot" comes from the expression *abba*.

The basis of any specifically *Christian* authority in a community must be the imitation of Christ. Authority-figures can only call upon this criterion as they summon their communities, as individuals or as a group, to live the Gospel imperative of obedience. Obedience, in response to a Christian authority, must be seen and understood by all concerned as a fundamentally important aspect of our mission, to continue in history the living presence of Jesus of Nazareth. This sounds very idealistic indeed, and may seem to place far too much stress on the responsibilities of the authority-figure. Two further issues need to be clarified at this stage.

a) No authority figure re-incarnates Christ, as all are sinners. However, the ideal is that all authority-figures see their primary task, within the context of their particular community, as an ongoing mission to act as a central figure, through a quality of life, reminding the people with whom and for whom they live of the ultimate significance of the obedience of Jesus of Nazareth.

b) Any authority-figure who attempts to thus exercise authority without a community which shares such ideals, and which understands the role and function of authority and obedience in a community in this way will soon come to grief. In other words, the possibility for re-living the Christian model for genuinely *Christian* authority and obedience will only be found in a com-

> munity which is deeply committed to Christian values. This is where a great number of experiments to live such a form of authority and obedience have failed. The superiors appointed have often done well, but the communities were not prepared to open themselves to the risk of the radical life-style of Jesus of Nazareth. However, it was generally the superior who was blamed for the failure.

I believe that the Pauline ideal of authority in the Christian community acts as a force to draw the community together, in an attempt to constitute the whole Christ. As someone earnestly strives, on a full-time basis, to present the community with the living reality of the challenge of Jesus to each one of them to go further and further away from him or herself into the mystery of God, that person becomes the head towards whom all look in hope. This figure helps us to make sense of the hum-drum of the everyday work in which we are involved, shows us that success at that level is not ultimately the touch-stone of our value to the community, and makes clear — not only in words, but especially in his or her person and function within the community — what our life is really all about: a radical openness to God our Father, in imitation of Jesus of Nazareth, Son and Son of Man. Paul himself never speaks of an obedience to the will of God, and he never speaks of an obedience to any form of "law". He speaks only of obedience to Christ (II Cor. 10,5-6) or to the Gospel (Rom. 10,16; Gal. 2,14; 5,7). These two (Christ and the Gospel) are, in reality, one and the same, as the preaching of the Gospel through word and quality of life is the continuation of the presence of Christ down through the centuries. Paul thus is speaking of an obedience which is faith. The two coalesce as our lives of obedience are the touchstone of our "life in Christ", our imitation of him, cost what it may. Obedience, therefore, is where we touch the *person* of Jesus, and where we show the world that we have allowed Jesus to touch our lives. Obedience is a total commitment of the believer to the following of Jesus of Nazareth.

There is even more to it, as we believe, along with St. Irenaeus (who died about 180), that those of us who are prepared to let everything go and commit ourselves totally to Christ will ultimately be those people most fully alive: "God's glory is in living men and full life for men is in the vision of God" (*Adversus Haereses* IV, 20,7). We are convinced that we will be fully human only when we are fully Christian, and that we will be fully Christian only when we are fully human. The two realities are inextricably intertwined. We must be careful, in our use of this great passage from Irenaeus, not to trip off the pat phrases which are so popular, and on the lips of everyone, without being prepared to see and live out the consequences of such expressions. A fear-ridden individual who has to be protected from all decision making by a strong superior is obviously not fully human, suffering from that loss of a God-given will of which we spoke earlier. Such a person cannot claim to be living a fully Christian life. There is, however, the other side of this story. There are many who, in the name of a "new freedom" wish to do their "own thing" at all times. Here we are faced with a serious loss of the sense of the cross in the Christian life, of the imitation of Christ who, "though he was in the form of God, did not count equality with God a thing to be grasped, but emptied himself, taking the form of a servant" (Phil. 2,6-7). Obviously, such a person can hardly be called fully Christian, as he or she has lost touch with a central element in the following of Jesus. When this happens — following St. Irenaeus to his logical conclusion — there is a subsequent loss in the fullness of that person's humanness. Thus the commitment to obedience becomes our means to the fullness of life, the fullness of Christianity and the fullness of humanity. Authority has the tremendously difficult task of creating a situation where this can happen; a situation where a Religious can make a fully human and a fully free decision to commit him or herself continually to the imitation of Christ. If this situation exists, by what right does a Religious refuse obedience? If it is lacking, by what right does a Religious superior demand obedience. Leonardo Boff has put it well:

> The problem of obedience lies in the freedom that disposes me to do another's will. The motivation for this is not the will of the other, which gives rise to a kind of legalism. It is the free "I" who determines this myself for the sake of God, and not solely or simply for the sake of the superior. *Obedience is thus synonomous with pure freedom understood as full control over oneself.* Only those who know how to give orders to themselves are capable of obedience. Those who can do this possess authority; they grow and help others to grow.
> Obedience, then, has nothing to do with the selfishness and passivity of people who submit to everyone in order to avoid having to think or make decisions of their own. Obedience is the greatest free decision one makes for God (*God's Witnesses in the Heart of the World*, p. 149. Stress mine).

The Practice of Obedience

The radical nature of the biblical message is clear, but when we turn to look at the working out of this model of obedience in our lives the difficulties arise. The message is of the upward call into Christ (see Phil. 3,4), leaving totally free the individual's initiative and responsibility, exercised, however, within the context of a total dedication on the part of both the individual and the community to the imitation of the life-style of Jesus of Nazareth. Once we see our obedience in this way, then we are working in the area of God's mysterious gifts of grace, both in the gift of the person of Jesus, and then in the gift of the free, though at times sinful, response of the Christian to the gift of Jesus. This, of course, is very difficult to *control*, and thus open to abuse and subsequent criticism. Our more traditional forms of Religious obedience left little to chance, errors were quickly identified, causes eliminated and confusion was reduced to a minimum. It would be foolish to think that in the situation which I have attempted to portray as the ideal mistakes would be avoided. While such a situation should produce many authentic decisions, it will not exclude the possibility of mistakes. As a rule we like to avoid mistakes; we prefer to have everything in order, under control at all times, and obedience has often been used by superiors as a weapon to make sure that this happens by lopping off any initiative which may appear to be a threat to the established order. The Religious also used his obedience in the same way. There was never any risk of being personally responsible for mistakes, as one could always claim to "have permission". As everything was done under obedience, if anyone was at fault it was the superior, who gave the permission in the first place. Although this attitude to authority and obedience has already been greatly revised, and much progress has been made, it appears to me that we must push on with our re-assessment of this central aspect of the Religious and Christian life. We need to look carefully at two areas.

a) We need to review our attitudes to the notion of a superior: who they are, how we choose them, and what we expect from them. Behind this review must stand the word of Jesus:

> You know that those who are supposed to rule over the Gentiles lord it over them, and their great men exercise authority over them. *But it shall not be so among you*; but whoever would be great among you must be slave of all. For the Son of Man also came not to be served but to serve and to give his life as a ransom for many (Mark 10,42-45).

This means, in practice, that many of the criteria which have commonly been used for the appointment of superiors should be revised. Often a superior has been chosen because he or she has a strong personality, because he or she knows all about building construction, or is able to handle hospital administration or a lay staff in a college. As is quite obvious, these criteria have been used because the Religious life has been seen and understood primarily as being concerned with "getting a job done". Religious are a work force in the Church, and the people who have all the necessary secular skills and training have been appointed to make sure that the job is done well. Gone is all sense of the "mystery" of the phenomenon of a prophetic presence living in the heart of the Church, questioning the Church itself through its radical commitment to Gospel values. As is obvious, the primacy in the life of a Religious community must be shifted away from its being a work force into the area of its challenge to the Church and the world to take seriously the upward call into Christ. Surely the "tasks" could be shared throughout the community, for a mutual enrichment and sense of shared responsibility which will nourish the all important sharing which produces "life in Christ". However, the responsibility for the challenge of a personal one-to-one encounter with the radical call to lose oneself in love as we respond to the call to live as Jesus of Nazareth lived cannot be reduced to a shared ideal. While the sharing of life and ideals in a genuine Christian community will always spur us on, since the event of the Incarnation the modality of the challenge has necessarily become a "flesh and blood" experience. This is an important *theological* principle which stands behind some quite *practical* conclusions. Superiors are not just facilitators in a work force. They are theologically necessary for the continuation of the "incarnational" challenge of Jesus of Nazareth within a community publicly vowed to follow him. There must be an historical personality whose task it is to challenge the members of the community with the values and the life-style of Jesus of Nazareth.

b) Perhaps even more importantly, we need to undertake a more serious renewal in ourselves, to recapture our understanding of life primarily as something that makes sense because of our commitment, in faith, to a Christian community. At the very centre of our lives there should be a deep desire to be called further and further away from ourselves into the fullness of life which can be had only in the imitation of Jesus of Nazareth.

If we can work at these two tasks, then I believe that our obedience within our communities will become a sign in the world, a genuine instrument of evangelisation where the members are seen to be maturely responsible, but totally dedicated to "life in Christ". The witness value of our communities depends upon their being a setting where the members are seen to be mature human beings who are able to make decisions regarding their own lives. The usual objections will be made that this leads to chaos, and we must admit that this has, to some extent, happened in recent years. Far too often, however, we merely criticise such a phenomenon, without looking seriously enough at the real reasons why such things happen. One of the important reasons for some of the disorder which we have experienced is that so many of us have been trained in a certain form and understanding of obedience that we are too immature to adapt to the more biblical idea of obedience and authority offered us by the Church and by our own congregational chapters. We either reject it and withdraw from the risk of evangelical obedience, or we abuse our new-found freedom by behaving irresponsibly, like little children just let out of school. Now, twenty years after the Council, another problem arises regularly. In the "unclear" period of the recent past many of us have firmly established ourselves in our little "kingdoms", some of them outstanding works of charity which merit the praise of many. However, some of these "kingdoms" and special apostolates are totally under our own *control*, and we are loath to let go. A sincere imitation of the life-style of Jesus of Nazareth must question all this.

Any superior, even in a situation where the ideals outlined above are working, will on occasion have to act authoritatively. There will be times where they will have to intervene — as Paul did. What does one do when an individual or a community decides to turn away from the quality of the obedience of Jesus of Nazareth, thus becoming a negative sign in the Church? We know that Paul gave a considerable number of specific directives. He was well aware that he sometimes needed to enter a discussion with vigour. Some interesting facts emerge from a close study of these Pauline interventions.

a) When Paul intervenes he does not do so on his own authority, but to call his converts back to the Lord. This is very clear in those passages where he goes to considerable trouble to distinguish what comes from the Lord and what is his own opinion. We have already seen an excellent example of that practice in our consideration of I Cor. 7 (see a further example in I Thess. 4,1-12). This shows very well where Paul finds the source for his authority. He is never issuing a call to life because of the knowledge or intrinsic authority of Saul of Tarsus, but only in so far as he is catching up in his teaching what was taught by the Lord. Thus, he has his authority only in so far as he calls people to be imitators of him, as he is of Christ.

b) Paul never makes the final decision. He presents a teaching and states what is to be done in the light of their new life in Christ. This is particularly clear in the situation of the incestuous relationship discussed in I Cor. 5. The community appears to be quite prepared to allow such a relationship to continue, but Paul turns to the mystery of the death of Christ as he shows that the "newness" of their present life "in Christ" cannot tolerate such a situation (see especially I Cor. 5,6-8). Once he has made this teaching clear, and founded in the paschal mystery, he then leaves it to the community and the person involved. They must decide for or against the word, person and teaching of Jesus (see vv. 4-5 and 11-12). If the public rejection of Jesus continues, then Paul has no hesitation in recommending that the sinner be expelled from the community, but this expulsion is to be a salvific punishment: "that his spirit may be saved in the day of the Lord Jesus" (v. 5).

It is here that the rules and constitutions of Religious congregations and the directives of superiors find their value. They are an attempt to re-incarnate and to re-present in a contemporary situation, the words, message, person and demands of Jesus of Nazareth. Ultimately, this means that they are to call the Religious to a life which is outstanding in the quality of its love. This was the way of Jesus of Nazareth, and it is the way his followers must go if they wish to show to the world that their obedience renders them authentically human. Many contemporary Religious need to look carfully at this question. All orders and congregations have worked through long and tedious post-Conciliar chapters — and all the work which makes such chapters possible — to produce renewed Rules and Constitutions. Most of them are magnificent, and they truly reflect a great deal of the biblical and theological insights which I have attempted to elaborate in this book. But Religious, often still suffering from a "hang-over" in the aftermath of a rejection of the "old Rule" which they had to learn by heart and try to live to the letter, will have nothing to do with their new documents. This is tragic, and must be seen as such. Our Rules and Constitutions, along with directives from our superiors, are major ways in which Jesus is present to us with his demands. These demands may sometimes be a little "messy", and not be exactly what we are looking for . . . but so was the Incarnation "messy", and Calvary was certainly not what Jesus of Nazareth was looking for (again, see Mark 14,36).

Our earlier study of the obedience of Jesus did not produce some strange sort of character who was separated from our experience and thus distant from us. Jesus, like each one of us, experienced the whole gamut of human emotions and temptations. The difference between Jesus and us is that he never failed in his obedience. Again the letter to the Hebrews says it well:

> For we have not a high priest who is unable to sympathise with our weaknesses, but one who in every respect has been tempted as we are, yet without sinning (Heb. 4,15).

Jesus' sinlessness, however, did not arise from his being some sort of "angel", but from his radical and never-failing obedience. We sometimes hear it said that the newer Christologies have their value in showing that Jesus was human like us. That is not quite correct. In his perfect obedience and in his preparedness to go further and further away from himself down God's way in faith, hope and love, in his freedom to accept a future which only God could create, Jesus of Nazareth alone was the *perfect* human being. He has made sense out of humanity, while we, in our sinfulness, egoism, selfishness and desire to control, are always *less than human.* It is not by chance that Dan. 7 presents the enemies of Israel, those opposed to God's way in the world "like beasts", while the perfect Israel, the "holy ones of the Most High", radically open to the ways and the will of God, is summed up in "one like a son of man" (see Dan. 7,13-14). What is demanded of us is that we become more and more human, as we move closer and closer to the quality of the love and obedience of Jesus of Nazareth, Son and Son of Man.

Returning to the working out of this within the concrete Religious community, the response of each member of a community, one must be realistic about the difficulties and tensions created by such a radical life-style. A situation where a superior decides every issue because of his or her insights or, worse still, because of some vested authority which gives power over the lives and loves of others, must be avoided. We must continue to reach decisions together. Many of us feel that the interminable community meetings, house councils and provincial chapters have gone on for too long, and we are weary of them. This is an understandable but dangerous attitude. We must continue to face the hard work of these interminable meetings, as only in this way can we hope to come to some sort of light *together.* The way from Pilate's praetorium to Golgotha must have also seemed interminable to the cross-laden Jesus, but that journey led to a resurrection. Nevertheless, having said all this, there will always be some situations where the superior will need to make decisions, and these will cause anguish, pain, and real suffering. There can be no realistic theology of obedience unless this be taken into account. A painless theology of obedience must be a false one. But if, behind these difficult and painful situations, we have a community which is ultimately based on love, then the problems which arise are not insurmountable. In a context of loving authority and loving obedience, no error on the part of superior or subject will be irreparable, and this is another area where contemporary Religious life needs to examine its conscience. A lack of preparedness to accept error is a sign of a lack of love!

Despite all our care in the selection and appointment of superiors, and our shared dedication to the way of Jesus of Nazareth, the situation may still arise where a superior after due consultation and discussion — or sometimes because of a lack of it — makes a poor decision. What is the situation of the Religious who *knows* that this is the case, but who is still asked by the superior to abide by that decision? Here we must be careful with our terminology once more. I have no doubt that the Religious who is prepared to lay his or her life on the line in accepting a poor decision from a superior is living a Christ-like life. This is certainly and obviously a part of the way of Jesus of Nazareth, but is it a part of Christian authority and obedience? I think not. It may well be part and parcel of our lives, and I hope that such attitudes are common among Religious, but the Christian view of authority and obedience must be a positive and joyful common commitment to the life-style of Jesus. To accept suffering inflicted by the poor quality of life or the poor decision-making of another can *certainly* be a part of Christian living — but it must *never* be seen or explained as a function of the vow to Christian obedience.

The Function of the Vow of Obedience

The vowed life of obedience is touching the very heart of the Christian response, as we all attempt to follow the life-style of Jesus of Nazareth, Son and Son of Man, caught up in the mysterious presence of the active reign of God. He was totally directed by the will of God his father, cost what it may. All Christians are called to this form of life, and they are not challenged by a mere "idea", but by a man. Since the Incarnation the Church has rendered "incarnational", through all her fallible and essentially human elements, the call to obedience. She has the mission to present the challenge of the word and person of Jesus of Nazareth to men and women of all ages, in all their concerns.

Turning from the ideal to the signs of the times, there are two problems which I would simply like to point out.

a) The immediately obvious one, that men and women (from the earliest times) have tended to tear themselves away from God in a profound desire to *control*, to be the absolute masters of their own destiny. How well this tragedy was described in the ninth century B.C., in the pages of Genesis 1-11. There is little need for me to list the continued arrogance and egoism which are so much a part of our contemporary society, reflecting a deeply rooted movement away from the creating, calling Exodus God to whom man must never dictate terms, if he wishes to be truly human, truly all that God made him to be in the first place.

b) Closer to home we find a terrible danger within our own Church. As the historical, human institution of the Church is made up of men and structures, she will always be exposed to the risk of losing sight of the fact that she exists to call all men and women to "life in Christ" through the ministry of Christ's word and sacrament. The Church must *never* consider herself as an end in herself. When the administration centres begin to think that they have the whole mystery of the life of Christ in his Church under their exclusive control, then the very sense of our existence as the Church founded by Christ is put into jeopardy. Jesus did not found a group of disciples to *control* God's kingdom. He called them to "follow" him, and to call others to pursue that same journey, to fall, out of control, into the hands of a loving and jealous God, as he leads them into *his* future. Little wonder that the Council spoke of the need for a Church which is "at the same time holy and always in need of being purified" (*Lumen Gentium*, 8).

Religious obedience, lived out in the heart of the Church, is the obedience of a prophet. We must be seen as living under the divine urgency to go away from ourselves, and to lose ourselves in the mysterious plan of a mysterious God. In this way we will continue to proclaim to the people among whom we live, the freedom which a radical openness to God can create. We will also act as a thorn in the side of an over-confident, over-organised, over-institutionalised Church. The quality of our free but obedient lives must keep posing the question to our Church: Just why were you — the Institution — instituted in the first place?

> The profession of the evangelical counsels (!), then, appears as a sign which can and ought to attract all the members of the Church to an effective and prompt fulfilment of their Christian vocation ... The religious state reveals in a unique way that the kingdom of God and it overmastering necessities are superior to all earthly considerations. Finally, to all men it shows wonderfully at work within the Church the surpassing greatness of the force of Christ the King and the boundless power of the Holy Spirit (*Lumen Gentium*, 44).

Conclusion

I believe that the so-called crisis of authority is a myth. The considerable amount of disarray we have experienced in the Religious life in recent years is not coming from a contempt for authority. I think that there is an innate feeling among people who read the Gospels that an authority which rules by law and rod is not a *Christian* authority. What we want is real leadership, and that is hard to find ... and even harder to practise if you happen to be the one found! We will never succeed unless we are *all* convinced that we are *all* called to the one task: to reproduce in history a quality of a life of love which will make the world ask: "What do these people have which makes them what they are? Why do we not have it?" When the quality of life within our communities is raising such questions, then perhaps authority will have a real chance to lead us continually towards Christ, and we will have a means at our disposal to point to the person of Jesus of Nazareth as a way of life, and not just an interesting personality from the dusty pages of history.

We are living in an era of great opportunity and great light, and not in a time of crisis. However, the responsibility for the return to an authority and a life of obedience based on Gospel values lies squarely on the shouders of each one of us. The final Apostolic Exhortation of Pope Paul VI spoke about the evangelising force of the Religious life in the Church. In many ways, the late Holy Father's words sum up all that I have been trying to say.

> Religious, for their part, find in their consecrated lives a privileged means of evangelisation.

It is in our poverty, chastity and obedience, in our consecrated lives, that we find a privileged means of effective evangelisation. How? The Pope goes on to explain how it functions:

> At the deepest level of their being they are caught up in the dynamism of the Church's life, which is thirsty for the divine absolute and the call to holiness. They embody the Church in her desire to give herself completely to the radical demands of the Beatitudes. By the quality of their lives, they are a sign of total availability to God, the Church and the brethren (*Evangelii Nuntiandi*, 69).

This will only happen if the life of each one of us commands respect and asks questions of the world and the people among whom we live. To do this we have to be fully mature Christians, seen to be making fully mature decisions which draw us deeper and deeper into the mystery of Christ and his Church. Our communities exist to give us this opportunity. It will only happen, however, if the ideal which calls this community into existence, Jesus of Nazareth, is re-incarnated in the person of the leader who is the symbolic centre without whom true community in the Christian sense is impossible. But the leader can only be so if the community governed is totally taken up with the values of Christ, committed to the task mapped out for us by the Word of God:

> It is no longer we who live, but Christ who lives in us; and the life we now live in the flesh we live by faith in the Son of God, who loved us and gave himself for us (see Gal. 2,20).

EVANGELICAL IMPERATIVES

The world in which we live finds it easy to ridicule any suggestion that such unfreeing things as poverty, chastity and obedience could be regarded as the keys to a unique freedom and a unique opportunity to love and to be loved. I hope that I have shown that the ridicule of the world is hollow indeed, and that the hollowness of the ridicule comes from the world's inability to really understand freedom, and to really understand love.

There has only been one genuinely free person in the history of mankind: Jesus of Nazareth. His freedom arose from his profound openness to God, an openness which led him further and further away from the criteria of a worldly success story, into a human failure. It is here that the world is unable to see the real issue, because it will not admit its ultimate need for resurrection. Unable to go outside its categories of achievement and success stories — things that can be measured in terms of human criteria and controllability — Jesus of Nazareth must be judged a failure. Many pay him a lip service, and even occasionally attend a Church function ... but the God they adore is found on different altars. Our contemporary society will also judge as a failure anyone who follows Jesus of Nazareth along the same way of a total gift of self in love, a love which frees and does not possess, lit up only by the misty but powerful hope that this sort of love makes sense of life.

We hear on all sides that we are made slaves by our poverty, our chastity and our obedience. The problem which needs urgent attention, however, is that many of us have allowed this criticism to develop by the poor quality of the freedom and the love in our own lives. In some ways we can tend to become slaves. To caricature a possible attitude: poverty means no money, chastity means no love and obedience means no decision making. Naturally, we scoff when we hear the vowed life spoken of in that fashion, but is there not a grain of truth in it? Are there not some among us who are looking for the wrong kind of freedom: a freedom from a deep commitment to mankind and God's purposes of salvation for the world which can only be discovered through a critical but loving involvement with the world? It is my experience that there are many Religious who see their commitment to the Religious life as an escape from the risks of such an involvement, and who consequently understand their poverty, chastity and obedience as the means by which such an escape is effected. Is this not a form of slavery?

It appears to me that one of the most effective ways to right this wrong within the Church is to show that poverty, chastity and obedience are not the unique privilege of a small group of specialists who have somehow separated themselves from the rest of humankind. It is urgently important for all Religious to see that they have not been called to a "better" form of the Christian life, but to a "different" form of that life, and that despite the differences, we are all caught up in an attempt to follow the poor, chaste and obedient Jesus of Nazareth. Somewhere along the line this all-important and obvious truth has been forgotten, to the detriment of all — not only the Religious, but also the non-Religious, who have tended to accept the tradition: if the Religious life is a "better" form of the Christian life . . . then their Christian lives are somehow "second-class".

How has this happened? As I mentioned in the Preface to this book, we have lost touch with the supreme norm of all Christian life: Jesus of Nazareth as he is portrayed in the Gospels. To be sure, there is a great deal of christological debate going on among the scholars these days, with all sorts of aggressive assertions and counter-assertions providing good press for *Time Magazine.* But what of the challenge of this man to the everyday Christian who cannot even afford to purchase Küng, Schillebeeckx, Rahner, Kasper and Boff; let alone understand them when they read them? They are subjected to the ravings and the rantings of the various defenders of either the new thought or the old, and what is happening to the vital life-giving presence of the challenge of Jesus of Nazareth in the meantime? It is here that the Religious must begin to ask themselves questions. They have not been called to a "better" form of Christianity, but they have responded publicly to a public witnessing of the person and message of Jesus of Nazareth, to make the challenge of poverty, chastity and obedience a life-giving force in the Church and the world of today.

There are many reasons why the Religious life is an important feature of the contemporary Church. Here I would like to point out again that through all the polemics and confusion, the Church needs to be questioned by the quality of the life of a free and loving group of people in her midst, which sees as its *primary task* the continuation of the free and loving life-style of Jesus of Nazareth, cost what it may. Our poverty, our chastity and our obedience are not a privileged possession which set us apart from the Church and the rest of the world. Biblical poverty, chastity and obedience are the vocation of every man and woman, and they are, I hope I have indicated, our way to authentic humanity. It must be so, as through such a life-style we follow the poor, chaste and obedient Jesus of Nazareth along a path which leads to the ultimate answer to the deepest longings of the hearts of all men and women: resurrection.

More than that one cannot say, or ever hope to say. The world will continue to ask: "What is freedom?", and even more insistently, "What is love?". But the answer will not be found on the lips of the philosophers. It can only be found by looking again to Jesus of Nazareth, and by taking the risk of reproducing that same freedom and that same love in our own lives, as we follow him down his way.

Why can we do no more? Why is it impossible to be more explicit about the exact nature of the greatness to which all men and women have been called? William H. Vanstone provides the answer:

> We are describing not that which any man has known or experienced but that towards which every man, at the depths of his being which is more profound than language, gropes and aspires (*Love's Endeavour, Love's Expense*, pp. 53-54).

A Select Bibliography

With this short list I would like to indicate a few further books and articles which an interested reader may find helpful. I am also providing here the full bibliographical details of most of the works I have cited. There were a few citations taken from other authors, not mentioned here. Full details were given for their books within the text itself.

Boff, L., *God's Witnesses in the Heart of the World*, Religious Life Series 3 (Chicago/Los Angeles, Manila, Claret Center for Researches in Spirituality, 1981.)

Connor, Paul M., *Celibate Love* (London, Sheed and Ward, 1979).

Metz, J. B., *Followers of Christ: The Religious Life and the Church* (London, Burns & Oates, 1978).

Moloney, Francis J., *Disciples and Prophets: A Biblical Model for the Religious Life* (New York, Crossroad Books, 1981).

Moloney, Francis J., "Matthew 19,3-12 and Celibacy. A Redactional and Form Critical Study", *Journal for the Study of the New Testament* 2 (1979) 42-60.

Murphy-O'Connor, J. and Others, *What is Religious Life? A Critical Reappraisal* (Dublin, Dominican Publications, 1977; Wilmington, DE. Michael Glazier, 1979).

Raguin, Y., "Chastity and Friendship", *Supplement to the Way* 19 (1973) 105-117.

Rahner, K., *Religious Life Today* (London, Burns & Oates, 1977).

Rees, D. and Others, *Consider your Call: A Theology of Monastic Life Today* (London, SPCK, 1978).

Tillard, J. M. R., *The Gospel Path: The Religious Life* (Bruxelles, Lumen Vitae, 1977).
Tillard, J. M. R., *There are Charisms and Charisms: The Religious Life* (Bruxelles, Lumen Vitae, 1977).
Williams, H. A., *Poverty, Chastity and Obedience. The True Virtues* (London, Mitchell Beazley, 1975).
Vanstone, W. H., *Love's Endeavour, Love's Expense. The Response of Being to the Love of God* (London, Darton, Longman & Todd, 1977).

INDEX TO BIBLICAL REFERENCES

Old Testament

JOB

PSALMS

QOHELETH

ISAIAH

JEREMIAH

EZEKIEL

DANIEL

HOSEA

MICAH

AMOS

ZEPHANIAH

ZECHARIAH

New Testament

MATTHEW

MARK

LUKE

JOHN

ACTS

ROMANS

I CORINTHIANS

II CORINTHIANS

GALATIANS

EPHESIANS

PHILIPPIANS

COLOSSIANS

I THESSALONIANS

II THESSALONIANS

HEBREWS

I PETER

I JOHN